No More Procrastination!

No More Procrastination!

Get Into Action,
Achieve Your Goals!

Compiled by
Leslie Ann Cardinal, M.Ed.

The Cardinal Success Book Series

Disclaimer

The opinions expressed in this book are not a guarantee of results, because your results are determined by your own efforts and decisions. The ideas and opinions in this book are not meant to take the place of legal, tax, medical, or other professional advice. If you need advice, please seek the help of a qualified professional.

Thank you for purchasing this book!

It is our goal to share resources that help you achieve your professional and personal success. There are special free resources to help you in your quest to eliminate procrastination and get things done. To receive them, go to

http://TheProcrastinationBook.com

We would love to hear about your successes with conquering procrastination!

Dedication

This book is dedicated to my friend and mentor, Connie Ragen Green. Connie shows by her example what is possible in the realm of creating a successful online business from the ground up. Her patience, step-by-step teaching, and continued encouragement have made a big difference in my life as I add new dimensions to my business and my life.

Thank you, Connie!

Contents

Foreword

By Steve Arensberg

I could easily make the joke about waiting until the last minute to write this foreword for this book on procrastination—it would be trite, certainly, but would also be true. (And it wouldn't really be funny. Okay, maybe a little bit.)

My first meeting Leslie was a gift—literally. My former boss, Sally, presented us with the gift of a one-on-one coaching session with Leslie (or a subscription to the Harvard Business Review—no question which of those choices was the better one, and has continued to be...).

And that literal gift has become an amazing ongoing gift of support and friendship, and sometimes commiserating on the topic of procrastination.

Leslie, my wife Jen, and I have all struggled with our own versions of procrastination over the years, and we've offered each other support as we've struggled to find a process and a mindset that helps us overcome those challenges.

We all (including you, dear reader) have reasons for procrastinating that are deeply personal, rooted in our own psychologies, and as difficult to understand as any deep part of ourselves. Truly knowing ourselves means knowing and embracing our challenges, our faults—including how and why we procrastinate. And we all do it, in some part of our lives.

And while talking about procrastination can be funny, particularly in all the bizarre and amazingly creative ways we find to avoid the work we really should be doing—the subject of procrastination, and the reasons we experience it, is serious. For all of those reasons are capable of keeping us from doing the things we deeply want to do, or feel called to do.

I'm so thankful to Leslie for creating this collection of personal stories and useful strategies for overcoming procrastination and actually accomplishing those things we want to do. Just one of these stories or techniques that Leslie has gathered has the potential to change a life for the better, breaking the dam that keep us stuck, and allowing the river of our lives to flow more broadly and strongly toward where it's meant to go.

I hope you find at least one anecdote or tactic or concept that resonates with you, and that its application to your own procrastination challenges allows you to accomplish that great work you're meant to do.

Steve Arensberg

Introduction

If you procrastinate, you are in good company!

When I told people that I was writing a book about procrastination, almost everyone smiled and offered to help by being a "case study" for the book because they often find themselves procrastinating. I had to laugh along with them, because procrastination has been an ongoing challenge for me as well. And that is why I began writing this book. I wanted to find practical, workable ideas and strategies to help reduce or overcome procrastination. And I knew that I wanted to share the ideas I found so that they could help you too.

Procrastination is something that virtually everyone struggles with, at least to some degree. I believe that this is because we live full lives in a time of great opportunity. It is easy to have far more options and possibilities and obligations than we will have time to complete. This puts us in the position of having to make choices and set priorities. Some of the items on our To Do lists are part of our jobs or businesses. Others are responsibilities that come along with having a family and a home and being part of a community. Some come from dreams or wishes that we want to pursue.

Regardless of the source of the things on our list, when we choose one item to work on, all of the other items on the list have to wait. And that is where procrastination starts. And it can get worse when there are things on the list that we need to do or that we must do, but that we don't really want to do. Or when there is a dream that we want to pursue but we put it off and procrastinate about it because it seems like we have so many required or urgent tasks that we need to do first.

I started this book because I want you to be able to pursue your dreams. I want you to be able to fulfill your key commitments and to feel a sense of success and accomplishment. Procrastination can be one of the big obstacles to achieving these goals. Because I find procrastination to be a challenge too, I knew I didn't have all of the answers for how to overcome it.

So I turned to a number of my colleagues to ask them to share their best ideas and strategies with me. If they were willing, I asked them to write a chapter for this book so that you could benefit from their experience and wisdom too. They have shared some tremendous advice and some outstanding strategies.

Each chapter is short and easy to read. I encourage you to read it in the way that will work best for you. You can start with the topics that most attract you. You can read a quick chapter each day and then try the ideas in your life. Or, you can dive in and read straight through, to benefit from all of the great ideas and strategies. Experiment with the techniques and see which ones work best for you.

I wish you wonderful joy and satisfaction in becoming more successful in handling procrastination and achieving your goals in your life. I would love to hear about your progress and your success as you work with the ideas and strategies!

Chapter 1
What Causes You To Procrastinate?

by Adrienne Dupree

According to Wikipedia, procrastination is "the avoidance of doing a task which needs to be accomplished. It is the practice of doing more pleasurable things in place of less pleasurable ones, or carrying out less urgent tasks instead of more urgent ones, thus putting off impending tasks to a later time." I am sure that all of us have procrastinated at some time or another. If this is a practice that you exercise frequently, then it can lead to major problems.

If there is something that you have been procrastinating about, take a minute to determine why you are procrastinating. Do you have some anxiety about the task? If so, acknowledge it and determine how you can get past it. Is it something that you truly hate to do? Is it something that you just don't want to deal with? Burying your head in the sand is not going to make it go away.

A lot of times, we put off the things that are unpleasant or we hate to do. We find a million reasons why we should do something else. For example, I hate going to the grocery store so

I will wait until there is literally no food in my house before I go. I would rather eat out instead of just going to the store. This really doesn't make rational sense. Currently, I am making a concerted effort to eat healthier; therefore, I need to eat at home more. I now have an incentive to go to the store. I am looking up recipes so I can have a variety of meals. Find some incentive for the things you have been procrastinating about. This will make it easier to get those tasks done.

Many times, children in school or even adults procrastinate when it comes to completing homework or projects. How many of us have experienced an all-nighter because we waited to the last minute to start on the project even though we knew about it well in advance? This leads to a lot of stress and anxiety. Many people will say that they work better like this. Is this true or just a rationalization for procrastinating? If you start on a project early, then you will have time to review it and make changes. Usually if you come back to something you have completed days earlier, you will find ways to tweak and improve it. Not only will you produce a better quality product but you will have reduced stress as well.

If you are an employee, your procrastination only goes on for so long. If there is a task that you are responsible for completing, then eventually, you have to do it. Your boss is expecting you to complete the tasks that you are responsible for. Your tasks have to be completed by the deadline you were given.

As an entrepreneur, we have to be self-motivating and responsible for our own actions. We do not have a boss making sure that we complete our tasks. We are our own boss. This is very liberating and exciting for most people but also means that you have to be accountable to yourself. Entrepreneurs need to complete all tasks that are required in order to have a successful business, not just the ones they enjoy. There is no room for procrastination in the world of an entrepreneur. You are in control of your own destiny.

There are several techniques that you can use to overcome procrastination. If there is a task that you truly hate, then try to delegate it to someone else if possible. Find someone who does not mind doing the task that you hate. It is a win-win situation for both of you. More than likely, they will do a better job at the task than you will. Another thing you can do is try the reward system. Reward yourself after you complete the task that you hate. Delay doing something you want to do until the task is completed. You will feel great after getting the task done.

Another way to battle procrastination is to make yourself do the tasks that you have been putting off first. In order to do the other tasks that you enjoy, you have to complete the other tasks first. This is a variation of the bribery method that parents use on their children sometimes. You have to eat your vegetables first before you can get dessert. You now have an incentive to complete those tasks that you have been procrastinating about.

Instead of trying to complete those tasks that you have been putting off all at one time, you could break the tasks into bite-size pieces. You may be putting off the task because you are overwhelmed. Take some time to determine the individual steps that are required to get the task completed. Schedule these little steps over time so that you feel some sense of accomplishment once you complete part of the task. By the time the task is due, you have completed it. Doing a little bit over time makes those tasks that you really don't want to do more bearable.

Having an accountability partner can decrease your procrastination tendencies. When you have made a declaration to another person that you are going to complete something at a particular time, you don't want to go back on your word. You are much more motivated to get the task done because you do not want to admit that you did not finish what you said you would finish. Personally, this has helped me. I have an accountability partner that I speak with during the week. Not only do we talk on a regular basis but we send each other a sheet outlining the tasks we are going to accomplish for the week. We also determine which tasks will be completed each day.

Our perception that the task needs to be completed perfectly also leads to procrastination. My need to know all of the details up front prevents me from just getting things done sometimes. As an analytical person it is very hard to function in the realm of "good enough". However, perfection can paralyze you and leads to nothing being accomplished. This does not mean that you produce something inferior but it does give you permission to go back later and make adjustments.

Lastly, doubt can lead to procrastination. Doubt can stop you dead in your tracks. You start to doubt whether you can achieve a goal that you have established. In order to avoid failure, you do nothing. When I first started with my Amazon business, I did not have the confidence that I could do it even though there were others who were very successful. I was afraid that I was going to make a mistake so the merchandise that I bought sat in my house for several months. Finally I realized that this thought process was ridiculous and I needed to just jump in. It was fine and I have had much success with my Amazon business.

Don't beat yourself up too much if you procrastinate. I believe that all of us do it from time to time. The goal is to recognize it and determine how to overcome it.

Adrienne Dupree is an author, online marketer, affiliate marketer, information product creator and also has an ecommerce business. Her company, Leave the Corporate World Behind, teaches people in corporate America who want to get out of the rat race, stop trading time for dollars and control their own destiny how to create an online marketing business that can replace their income. You can find out more about Adrienne Dupree and Leave the Corporate World Behind at http://leavethecorporateworldbehind.com.

Chapter 2
Procrastination is Like a Vitamin Deficiency

by Angela Woodrow

What if procrastination is like a nutritional deficiency? When you have a nutritional deficiency, it is a drain on your energy and your effectiveness. The same is true when procrastination happens. Your energy and efficiency are often diminished.

The good news: Procrastination can be decreased and in some cases eliminated.

The bad news: Fixing procrastination is not a once and done activity. Just like any good health care regime, it must be monitored and measured over time.

To get started, let me offer up a few definitions to think about. Define procrastination as having a fear or a perceived inability to accomplish something. Define fear as **F**alse **E**vidence **A**ppearing **R**eal. Think about deficiency as a drain on energy. And think about energy as a key part of effectiveness, efficiency and joy.

With these definitions in mind, there are a few general rules that will help decrease the procrastination-related deficiency.

First, you have to understand the root cause. What is draining your effectiveness and efficiency? Once you have figured out the root cause of the drain on your energy, you can come up with a regime or a routine to reduce or eliminate the procrastination. It can be just as simple as taking your vitamins. It may be as easy as that...and it is that hard.

If you are good at establishing a routine, then getting a handle on procrastination will be simpler for you. And yet, even when you are in a routine you can still be susceptible to drains on your energy. Deficiencies are tricky and hard to understand. This is especially true when you are always feeling drained, out of energy, and not having any joy for the process or the project.

For me, discovering I had a vitamin deficiency was a bit of a shock. I had always considered myself pretty successful with my diet. I liked fruits and vegetables. I ate them in great quantities. Sometimes my family accused me of being a rabbit. Imagine my surprise when I was told I had a vitamin deficiency.

My levels were so low that it required a few months of drastic measures to boost the levels to close to normal. I was glad to be feeling better after months of being tired and always feeling drained.

But after the initial burst of fresh energy from the treatment, I seemed to struggle again with low energy. Why was I not able to eliminate this deficiency? It was pointed out to me after a few rounds with various doctors that I had not uncovered the root cause of the deficiency.

So I immediately set about figuring out how I could reverse the drain on my energy. It was not an overnight process. I had to build some new dietary awareness and habits. But when I found the right combination of foods and vitamin supplements, my energy returned, my zest for life was back to its normal levels, and life was good again. I still have to get my vitamin levels checked regularly. My body's ability to absorb the vitamins can be thwarted by simple things like taking over-the-counter allergy medication, or trying a different brand of vitamins to save a few dollars on the monthly grocery bill.

Experiencing the vitamin deficiency has taught me to see and think about life on two levels: the micro level and the macro level. On the micro level, the nutrients I am eating help me use the nutrients in my body as effectively as possible. On the macro level, there are things I can do in my daily life to ensure that I help keep my energy levels well charged. This includes making sure my daily schedule includes time for exercise and for plenty of the right kind of sleep!

I am realizing that most of life's lessons are built on two concepts: 1) you make advances in understanding when you can relate them to earlier accomplishments or lessons learned and 2) when you are able to look at a problem with a new understanding and new thinking you are able to change your approach to achieve a different result.

As you begin to look at a solution to a problem with a new lens, the opportunity for change occurs. I really liked the results I achieved by thinking about my vitamin deficiency as an opportunity to change my diet to increase my body's ability to absorb minerals. I wondered if this approach to changing a habit could be applied in other areas of life.

Could I add a 'supplement' to my work life that would help me eliminate procrastination? Could I eliminate the drain on my energy and joy with a more effective and efficient thought process? Is it possible that by increasing my strengths, efficiency, and effectiveness, that I could reduce and eventually eliminate procrastination?

This thought process gave me a new lens to evaluate systems and processes that were draining my energy. I also realized that, just as with the first round of vitamin supplements, it worked for a short while, but did not work over a longer period of time. It required me to make more changes.

All change is hard. With my physical health, there were weeks of learning how to bake and create foods in a new way that would work better for me. And when I was not willing to pay the price at the grocery store for these items 'already prepared,' and I did not have time in my day to make them from scratch, I realized that I did not really need them in my diet. And so the process of deleting and eliminating some things from my diet freed my body and my budget. There are fewer of the old food choices that work for my health now. But, over time, I have also learned to like a few new foods. I realized that I really do not lack for taste or choice. The mindset has shifted!

I got really excited when I realized that I could apply these same thought processes to some of the pesky processes and systems in my business! By approaching procrastination like a vitamin deficiency I was able to see that the business changes that I needed to make were going to be things that would have to happen over a period of time. This mind shift was not as simple as just 'taking one pill.' No, just as eliminating the vitamin deficiency requires ongoing daily diligence plus new skills and habits to maintain my improved mood and energy levels, I realized that the same idea applies to addressing procrastination in my business.

As a businesswoman and coach, I am passionate about helping others achieve their goals. And yet I am a procrastinator around some of my own business processes and systems...you know those systems that help build and make a strong foundation for a growing business. These systems are necessary and can even be fun to set up. But maintaining and sustaining them is hard work.

There are also tasks that I avoid because I cannot see how to accomplish them. Other tasks require energy and effort that is not in my realm of fascination. I can make lists all day long and create great action plans, but often I find myself approaching these tasks and activities with delay and procrastination.

It is also easy for me to default to a mindset that I should take care of other people's needs first. This can be a good and worthy value but, when it is out of balance and blocks my effectiveness in running my business, it creates a drain on my energy and efficiency. And ultimately, this mindset drains my joy for my chosen field of work and vocation.

It takes hard work to maintain your health, your business, your relationships, or any other aspect of your life that is important. When I find myself putting things that are important to me at the bottom of the list and thinking that I will do them later when everyone else is asleep, I am really procrastinating! Not only does this cause a drain on my effectiveness as a businesswoman, reducing my sleep time also increases the risk that my physical vitamin deficiency could reoccur in my area of health.

This was a shock and a rude awakening when I began to see my work habits and myself in this light. Procrastination was a very significant deficiency in honoring my own work and health needs.

It has also taken years for me to get past the notion that things that happen smoothly for other people should also happen smoothly for me. And when they don't go as smoothly as I would like, I often avoid doing them. This is FEAR: **false evidence appearing real.** And this for me is a big part of my energy deficiency (also known as procrastination).

I finally realized that I needed a "vitamin supplement" for procrastination just as I do for my physical health! I needed to take my "vitamin D" so that I can appropriately Delegate, Delete, Do, or Defer the tasks on my list. I learned to review my work schedule through the new lens of these four "D" options.

My "vitamin D" supplement routine for business has helped me eliminate the "FEAR" and increase my energy and efficiency in business and in life. My "vitamin D" routine has created new joy in my life. You can use it too.

With actions that you may be procrastinating, you can choose any of the four "vitamin D" supplements below.

Delegate: have someone else do it.

Defer: does it really need to be done right now? If not now, when?

Delete: if it really does not need to be done, just bless it and release it and then delete it from your list.

Do it: take action and move forward!

The "Defer" option can have another level to it. I may choose to defer a task because the time is not right to do it now. But if I defer it, I no longer just vaguely assign it to some later time. The mindset shift is when I defer a task or activity, it becomes a scheduled appointment on the calendar that I do not change or miss.

"Defer" is like a filter for me. If a task keeps getting deferred, I realize quickly that it needs to be delegated or deleted. It is that simple. And it is that hard. Choosing to let something go is scary and freeing all at the same time. I have found when I choose to let something go, it often returns in a form that is more manageable. This frequently happens when someone else needs help with the same item and I am able to team up and share the work.

As you face your procrastination challenges, just remember to identify the root cause to the drain on your effectiveness and efficacy. You have to be willing to look at it through a new lens. Use your new "vitamin D" choices. As the mind shift occurs, your energy and effectiveness will increase and procrastination will decrease and could even be eliminated if you choose!

Angela Woodrow has been coaching and navigating change with individuals and organizations for over 15 years. She comes to the coaching conversation as a change advocate, with a passion for helping individuals find the right combination of tools and knowledge to chart a course of change with success and strength. Connect or contact Angie at www.thecoachingcontinuum.com

Chapter 3
Baby, I was Born This Way

by Cheryl Knight

When I started my role as a Human Resource Manager with a retailing company many years ago, I was surprised at the volume of phone calls from employees. All of them wanted my advice, needed help, or sometimes just wanted to complain. That was the job – to help with all of these. Many issues could be handled over the phone, but often it required getting in the car and driving to a store to see people face to face. Well, as you can imagine, with multiple stores having hundreds of employees each, the calls and corresponding issues were, at times, overwhelming. As time passed, I found there were certain types of calls I dreaded. So, as a result of being very busy and often not enthused by the topic, I began to delay returning some of the calls.

At first I felt a tiny bit guilty, you know - for procrastinating. Surely those employees felt their issues were important and required immediate attention. As I became more experienced in the role, I began to realize what I thought was either trivial, or at the least, a matter they should be able to solve on their own, usually was. Often by the time I did return those calls, the individual had already resolved the issue or had calmed down and realized they didn't need my assistance. So, I began to think of my procrastination as strategic procrastination.

I proudly shared my newfound approach with others, yet I often received responses like, "I would never let a call for help wait that long to return!" or "Don't you feel bad for making them wait?" And I realized NO, I didn't feel bad! And that made me wonder, "Is there something wrong with me?"

Years later I became certified to administer the Myers-Briggs Type Indicator® (MBTI®) personality inventory which helps people understand their innate preferences for, among other things, how they perceive the world and make judgements. What I learned is that I am a procrastinator by design. To quote pop singer Lady Gaga, "Baby, I was born this way!" What a relief this was to be freed from thinking I was not doing a good job just because I didn't take immediate action. What I clearly understood is given the passage of time, most things work themselves out.

Procrastination

Procrastination generally has a negative connotation and historically is defined as the putting off of important tasks to the detriment of the individual. Today, procrastination has taken on a broader meaning of simply not doing something right away. We may think, "I didn't get to it today....I'm a procrastinator." Or it's used as an accusation, "Why are you such a procrastinator? Just get busy and do it!" With this bad rap, it's easy to feel like a failure just because you don't do things right away or when others expect.

Another thing I learned through the MBTI® certification is why I perform well under deadline stress; my most creative juices really flow as time gets closer to the deadline. I know that most situations are flexible and invariably new information comes to light. This is why I don't like to complete tasks right away. We've all been there - the boss gives you a project and you work hard to get it done. Then the boss comes back with changes. Ugh! Now you have to either redo or undo the work you have already done. To the procrastinator by design, this is very frustrating. Time and time again, my perspective is validated--it's better to wait than to take immediate action. As a result, I don't feel bad or stressed for waiting to begin a project.

Now, this is not to say delaying action has never caused me problems – of course it's caused problems! More than once, I have waited until the last minute to work on a report and the computer acts up or the printer quits working. So yes, occasionally subpar work is submitted and deadlines are missed.

I don't want to overcome my innate preferences. I want to stay open to the possibilities of new information and changes. I want to keep my creative juices charged without feeling guilty. And, I still want to complete my work and activities on time. In my quest to do all of these, I have come to realize two things that have helped me tremendously. I must answer the questions, "Am I fired up about it?" and "Is it really a big deal?"

Are You Fired Up About It?

The first and most important question calls you to be sure the task is something you want to do. Are you excited about it? Is it important to you or to those close to you? Are there benefits to the task?

When you can tie an action or experience to the approach you like to use, the impact you want to have and to what you value most, it will exponentially increase the odds you'll take action. For the innate procrastinator, if you have a choice and you aren't fired up about it, why bother?

Now if you simply want to get better at basic things, such as paying your bills on time, the same approach works! To help you overcome procrastinating when there really isn't a choice, answer these questions:

1. How do you want to approach paying your bills? Do you view it as an unpleasant reality or as an important part of living a successful adult life? Could you pay the bills on a regular schedule either weekly or monthly? Would it make more sense for you to have "planned bill paying time" when each bill is due?

2. What is the impact of paying your bills? How does it create value for you? Does it enable you to provide nourishment for yourself and your loved ones? Do you value having a comfortable space to live, health insurance, transportation, electricity for light and air conditioning, and perhaps some extras too?

Yes, unfortunately, bills have to be paid and there are lots of other things we must do to live successful adult lives. So, find some meaning in those things and get fired up about it. Then, keep your answers close by or make a note card you can see when you sit down to pay your bills. Reminding yourself why you are fired up about it will keep you fired up about it!

Is It Really A Big Deal?

The second question to address is how long the task will really take. How big of a deal is it? In other words, is it something you can get done pretty quickly, or is there a lot to do over a set period of time? Thinking about what is involved, or if there are external factors that could impact success, helps you to decide if you need to get started now and pace yourself or if you can invoke your innate preference for procrastination.

A lengthy, multiple aspect task is really a project. And projects require thought and attention to ensure a timely and successful outcome. If you indeed are fired up about it, then sit down and think through the components of the project. There are several approaches you can take for this: brainstorming, mind mapping, and the to-do list. All three of these work well for the innate procrastinator and they are fairly unstructured and light on detail. Yea!

Brainstorming

Brainstorm a list of all things related to the project. Let's imagine you are planning a party and you want it to go smoothly without killing yourself in the process. Begin by making a list of everything you can think of in no particular order:

- Who to invite
- music
- what you want others to do
- food/menu/drinks
- location for the event
- invitations
- entertainment
- theme/attire
- date and time

Then group similar items together. For example, invitations and who to invite might be grouped together. Music and entertainment could be grouped together as well.

Once you have these groupings, you can see what's missing. For example, decoration is missing from the list. You can also decide what needs to be started now and what can wait.

Mind Mapping

Mind Mapping is a visual method that captures the major and minor tasks associated with a goal or project. As you think of tasks, determine the major tasks to reach the goal. Then link minor tasks to major tasks.

Mind mapping helps me visually to be sure all the tasks are captured. I can then decide where I need to take action quickly and what can wait until later.

There are programs, apps and websites for creating mind maps. You can also use a blank piece of paper and draw mind maps by hand.

The To Do List

Create an extensive to do list. Write down all the things you know are important. Be realistic in knowing that you will think of more things as time passes. Have someone else review your list to help you think of things you may have missed.

It is usually the last minute thoughts near the deadline that create havoc. A To Do List is the least structured approach, but is still a great way to capture all the tasks involved in your project or goal.

Bringing It All Together

Once you have your thoughts and ideas documented using one of these approaches, you can begin to plan. Now, if you are like me, an innate procrastinator, this is the hard part. I prefer to approach tasks when I am in the zone - when the mood strikes me. But that doesn't work very well for a project.

The non-procrastinator likely thrives on detailed plans - not so for the innate procrastinator. Rather than have a detailed plan for specific steps, what I have found most useful is to plan a regular time slot to accomplish something, anything, related to the project.

I am writing a chapter for a book and for a while I tried to write when the urge presented itself. I'm better when I can be spontaneous! After all, I have time before the deadline. But spontaneity gives legs to procrastination. The creative urge is almost always overcome by...well, life. As you might suspect, not much was getting written.

So now, I have one hour blocked off one day a week. In that time frame I focus on any of the tasks associated with writing. I could do research, writing, editing, or brainstorming. It is planned, yet spontaneous. Whatever action I take, I am making progress! It feels good to keep my weekly appointment and to see progress.

So if you have answered YES to "Am I fired up about it?" and "Is it really a big deal?" then choose your favorite approach to identifying all the aspects of the project. Then plan some regular time to be spontaneous in how you tackle the work.

There will always be those times when strategic procrastination serves a purpose. Realistically though, some things need immediate attention. Knowing the difference and using the tools that work for you will ensure success. Be clear on the approach you like to use, the impact you want to have, and what you value most. Decide where to begin and plan regular time so you can use deadline stress and its associated creativity. You can live in harmony with your innate procrastinator, and still complete things successfully and on time!

Cheryl Knight, PHR, is a Coach and Developer of Leaders within the retail business environment with over 20 years in the Human Resources and Leadership Development profession. Her passion is to help leaders learn more about themselves through assessments and feedback, gain clarity on their goals and aspirations, and then facilitate a process to accelerate their growth and development. Connect with Cheryl at https://www.linkedin.com/in/cherylkcoach.

Chapter 4
Keep on Track and Move Forward

by Cheryl Major

I noted that I need to write this chapter in BIG BOLD CAPS on my to-do list today, so I guess I've been procrastinating and should get down to it!

The above paragraph I wrote quite a few weeks ago; I now have to amend it as I just got a voicemail from Leslie telling me she needs my chapter in the next couple of days...oops.

Apparently procrastination is a subject I know something about.

First and foremost, a deadline, whether self-imposed or the one like Leslie just gave me really helps! Beyond that, I have three "tricks" I use to keep myself from procrastinating, or perhaps I should say to manage my procrastination.

Live and schedule today like I'm leaving for vacation tomorrow

Have you ever noticed how much you get done when you're going on vacation and can't kick the to-do list out to tomorrow? I've noticed it time and again over the years, and boy can I produce the day before I leave for vacation. I take great delight and relief in methodically checking off those items on my yellow legal pad!

I'm always amazed at the volume of work, the cleaning, the packing and the organizing I can accomplish when I'm under a deadline. This has been consistent enough that recently I've begun to look at what this means for me on a regular basis and how I can use this to my best advantage.

Warning: Sometimes I feel as though I need a vacation to recover from getting ready to go on vacation...

The getting ready for vacation approach requires the usual list, but I find I'm more apt to pay attention to it, not leave it behind, ignore it, or even lose it when I'm under the gun for vacation departure. My focus is sharper because I don't have the luxury of time to kick tasks to the next day. Usually I will be on a plane at that point.

Because I don't have the looming threat of the soon departing plane, using the "vacation" method does require self-discipline. It does work and when I focus on using it, I always have a significantly more productive day.

Don't think too much, just do

The second approach, "Don't think too much; just do" is key for me and for my personality. I never feel what I have done is ready for presentation. It needs more work, more tweaking, more practice to be good enough to put out there in the world. I don't know that I would call myself a perfectionist, but I am demanding of myself.

I remember when I was a student of piano, practicing was the key; I never felt I was ready for a performance. It was never good enough. It needed more work, or more practice, to be better.

As I've gotten older, I've recognized that is a pattern for me. It slows me down and keeps me in preparation mode rather than allowing me to do something, present it, and *then* tweak and revise to make it better. I never allowed myself to get past the initial step. It's hard to tweak, revise and make something better without a "finished" product to evaluate.

I held my first live event about six weeks ago. The advice I was given at the time by my business coach was to schedule it for a date no more than a couple of weeks out so I wouldn't have too much time to think about it. Wise words for me! I was under the gun to produce the product (the outline and Power Point slide presentation), rehearse a little and deliver in short order. That was a game changer for me.

At the end of the year, I decided to commit to writing 30 blog posts in 30 days. I didn't think too much about it. The thoughts I had went something like this, "What will I write about?" "What if I don't pull it off?" "Do I really need to tell people this is my goal and a commitment?"

Because I recognized the thought patterns that have held me back in the past, I decided to shut that down and just put it out there. I posted my commitment in a business Facebook Group and so far, so good. I will keep that commitment to myself.

Use a timer on my laptop for 30 minute work intervals

I have a timer on my laptop that I use, although not often enough (note to self to use it more). It's set to give me a work window of 30 minutes: 25 minutes to work and a "cool down" period of 5 minutes.

When I use it, I stay focused on the task at hand, but it also makes me aware of how quickly time passes when I'm focused on completing a task. I have a really boring task that I'm trying to complete to use a new contact management software program in my work. It's not something I can hand off to someone else because there are judgment calls based on the contacts involved that only I can make.

I have a goal to enter fifteen everyday so this task will get done by the end of the month. I use the timer and am amazed at how much time I spend trying to sort these fifteen contacts out and enter or delete from my database. If I weren't using the timer, I wouldn't have that awareness.

Procrastination is a challenge for most of us. I've known a few people who are so driven that I don't think they can spell or pronounce the word, but for the rest of us mortals, it remains to find the tricks and techniques that can keep us on track and moving forward to complete our tasks smartly and in good time!

Cheryl A. Major can be found on http://ThinStrongHealthy.com where she shares as she learns. Join us there; take what you can use now, and come back often to grow with the community as they teach themselves to eat well, love what they eat, and be happy! Live, love, laugh, and make Major improvements in your life!

Chapter 5
Procrastination is Resistance

by Connie Ragen Green

Whenever I think about procrastinating, I feel resistance from deep inside of myself to not move forward with the action I am avoiding. Even though I was committed to doing something specific at that moment in time because it was important to me, for some reason I would put it off and it would never be accomplished. Fortunately I have been able to overcome this feeling of resistance and my life has been forever changed.

This habit of procrastination has been with me since I was a child, yet as adults we are able to deal with these feelings in a very different way. As a little girl it seemed like I was in a constant battle to get things accomplished that were prescribed by and demanded from my parents, teachers, and other authority figures. I had little choice in the matter, so if I was asked to pick up my toys or take a bath or help with putting away the groceries I had to get moving and make it happen. When the teachers assigned homework, it was necessary to finish the task by the due date or face the consequences.

Once I was out of school and a part of the work force there were supervisors and bosses demanding that I do specific things as a part of my work day. If I even attempted to put off until tomorrow what was requested and due from me today, the domino effect took over and many people besides me were also affected. It was simply easier to sit down and get the work done in a timely manner so as to not make waves in my workplace. Over time some of these tasks became more palatable, but my resentment grew over the years as I came to feel as if the majority of my time was already accounted for by the people and the activities I was destined to be a part of in my daily life.

In 2005 I made the conscious decision to change my life completely. I left my former working life behind and became an entrepreneur. For the first time ever I was the sole decision maker when it came to how and when I would work on the various tasks that were required in the day to day running of my business. The concept of outsourcing made this so much better, as many of the activities that needed to be accomplished were better done by others, freeing up even more of my precious time.

Then one day it hit me square in the face; now when I procrastinated there was no one there to remind or scold me about what had still not been done. Half-finished tasks were left untouched and work piled up quickly. Days turned into weeks and my business stagnated. My lists of items that needed to be done got longer and longer, until finally I stopped writing things down and just waited until they were at a breaking point. This put me into "reactionary" mode where panic set in. At some point I even convinced myself that the act of "thinking" about what I would accomplish was the same as actually "doing" it. Not true.

I was drowning as a new online entrepreneur and no one was throwing me a life preserver. If I didn't do something right away to get back on track I would have no other choice but to return to the life I had abhorred for so many years, the life where other people called the shots and made decisions for me. It became my primary focus and goal to make sure my procrastination would never become an issue that would force me to take a job in order to pay the bills. That was more than I could face, so eliminating procrastination became my highest priority.

This called for drastic action on my part and I immediately sprang into action. I made a strict schedule for myself and blocked off my time in one hour increments. Next came a dynamic "to-do" list, in which I listed items that needed to be done in terms of their urgency and deadlines and then checking each one off as it was accomplished.

Returning to the habits I had once detested was the answer for me, because in order to enjoy my new freedom I now understood that structure and order was of prime importance. If an item remained on my list of daily tasks for more than two days, I took a closer look to see why this was occurring. Either it was something that actually did not need to be done at all or something I was not skilled at or interested in doing. My resistance to do certain things on a regular basis was my subconscious reminding me that my time is best spent on the tasks and activities I do best, and that everything else is best outsourced to people who can do these things in a far superior, and definitely more timely manner. In my business this included technology, bookkeeping, and graphic design. These were my areas of weakness and I wanted to focus only on my areas of strength so that my business would move forward more easily.

My resistance had kept me from taking the plunge and swimming towards the island. It kept me on the shore where I was safe and comfortable. Even though I kept insisting that I wanted a new and different life experience, my resistance kept me from allowing that to happen. While resistant my dreams remained just far enough out of reach as to not become my reality. It was like having a hard drive filled with viable projects and not being able to access them. It was painful and embarrassing and turned my daily life into nothing more than a mediocre existence. I had to take a stand and to refuse to entertain resistance ever again.

It has now been ten years since I came to the realization that procrastination is simply resistance creeping into our reality. Honor those feelings and you will soon be able to discern between meaningful tasks and those that hold far less value in the overall scheme of things.

Often I am asked if I have overcome procrastination in my life forever and my answer is always the same. I believe that we battle resistance and change on a daily basis and must work hard to keep it at bay. At least once a day I need to remind myself that "not feeling like it" is not a reason for not accomplishing a task or goal. And when I do take action and complete something I have set out to do, the taste is as sweet as honey. Do today what you might prefer to put off until tomorrow and you will experience this for yourself. It is the perfect example of having complete power and control over your destiny. It is a joyous feeling that you will learn to crave. I highly recommend it.

Connie Ragen Green is an author, speaker, and online marketing strategist living in southern California. As a former classroom teacher and real estate broker/residential appraiser, Connie left it all behind to come online in 2006 as an entrepreneur. Find out more at http://ConnieRagenGreen.com.

Chapter 6
Procrastination—The Cause, The Effect, and The Change

by Cynthia Charleen

A true procrastinator sees life as "Never do today what you can put off until tomorrow."

The Webster dictionary says that procrastination means "for tomorrow" and I agree with that. My own experience has been putting things off until a tomorrow that never actually comes. When I hear the phrase "Never put off until tomorrow what you can do today," I still hear the sound of my mother's voice, as I heard this sentence repeated many times when I wanted to postpone homework until later.

Which one are you--the do it now person, or the procrastinator? You can be a bit of both. I sometimes seem to slide into the procrastinator mindset with great intentions left behind. In my work as a personal organizer, I see the results of delay when I enter a client's home. Procrastination is actually decisions that have been postponed. It only takes a few of these delayed decisions to create a surrounding of clutter.

The Cause

We lead busy lives and there does not seem to be enough time in a day to do all that is needed. We rush into the house, grab a bite to eat, do a quick clothes change and leave for a meeting across town. It is tempting to not clean up as we go. Dishes may be left in the sink, clothes on the bed, shoes scattered around the room. What's a person to do with all this stuff?

Lack of time management can lead to procrastination. As productive time passes idly by, thoughts of putting things off often begin to seem more appealing. As more is left undone, the task list grows. Incomplete tasks become clutter on the desk and computer. There is so much to be done and so little time, or so it seems.

If any of this sounds familiar to you, here are a few quick tips to help you get control.

- Keep things simple. Have food prepared ahead that is tasty and nutritious. When time is limited, grab something that is simple to fix. Then take just two or three minutes to clear the evidence by putting dishes in the dishwasher or rinsing them off and setting them in the sink.

- Plan what you will wear and lay it out the night before. A good choice can be a basic outfit that can be dressed up or down according to what you are doing for the day. This works especially well for business days. The addition of a jacket and a change of shoes can change a simple outfit into a dazzler. This one idea can eliminate stress and procrastination so that your bedroom does not look like it exploded when you leave again.

- Take action now if a task can be done quickly. Little things postponed can become a cause of time delays as they add up to a big task instead of a small one. I have a rule that I don't put clothes back in the closet unless they are ready to wear. If a button is missing, sew it on promptly. If a shoe needs repair, fix it now rather than later.

- Hire someone to do the little things for you. This can be a big saver of time. If funds are limited, perhaps you can team up with neighbors and friends to share the tasks and save time. If each person does one of the tasks for all, then there is time available to do it now instead of putting off for a future date.

The Effect

Does fear of the unknown make you want to put things off until tomorrow? Few things get better by being ignored and the consequences can mount. For example, are you worried that you may owe more taxes? Ignoring them does make them go away. Problems can get larger with neglect until they can be devastating.

When financial records are not kept up to date, it can be costly. If you are required to file quarterly income statements and taxes, missing a couple of those can be a mounting problem. If you postpone filing employer taxes, you can be in even bigger trouble.

I know good people who have lost their retail business because they refused to handle issues until it was too late. Hiding one's head in the sand like an ostrich fails to provide much security or comfort for a business owner.

It may not seem like a problem to have things scattered and disorganized at home. However, these same habits will often show up in how you handle your business too. Is that a problem for you?

Postponed decisions in business can be costly. If some things are put off long enough, it may become too late to do them at all. If you have an opportunity to bid for a job or submit your ideas on a project, do it right away. You may receive extra consideration because it was submitted early. Project managers like the early bird who can help them get things done. It makes you both look good.

Please do not sacrifice quality of goods or services in order to do things faster. By planning ahead and implementing on a schedule, goals can be met and quality maintained. When you procrastinate, then it is tempting to rush to get caught up on what needs to be done instead of doing the normal quality that is expected.

The Solution

Do you want to stop putting things off and start getting more done? Here are some suggestions.

For big things like keeping good financial information, take a look at some of the financial software. Many accountants suggest Quicken or Quickbooks since they integrate with a central system that they can help you set up.

Yes, you can probably save money by doing this yourself. Determine a date and write it down in your calendar as a goal for when you will have your data entered, or will have someone else enter the information for you. Your accountant may have some contacts for people who can enter data quickly and you can put this task to rest.

Outsourcing is a way to clear away the barriers to being productive. It is my favorite suggestion to overcome the habit of putting things off until another time. Take the things that you do not want to do and find a person who has that interest and skill.

If you don't feel that funds are available in the budget for paid outsourcing of work, think of creative ways to share job responsibilities with someone who has the time and skill. It is important that they are reliable and can do the work well. For example, you may have a friend or colleague who enjoys working with social media postings and who would gladly trade those services for a few home cooked meals.

If you use Facebook, Twitter, or other forms of social media, best results are achieved with regular posting of ideas and opportunities for your audience to interact with you. You are at the heart of your business, so use your time to promote your work. Do it on a schedule. There are tools and resources online that enable planning in advance and acting consistently.

Make a plan that allows room for change but that has a basic structure such as a calendar that accounts for your time in quarter hour segments. Tracking your days like this will reveal where minutes are being lost that could be better used for productivity. Follow this regimen for 21 days and notice how much more you achieve.

Hootsuite has a free level of service available. Sunday night can be a good time to load the information to be sent out over the next week and then you can forget about having to post every few hours on social sites. Use simple tools like this that let you do some of the work ahead of time. This will help you gets things done faster and with less effort and certainly fewer postponed tasks.

In the book "The Miracle Morning" by Hal Elrod, I discovered ways to insure that my days would be consistent and productive when I apply the principles listed there. I encourage you to create your own miracle morning routine which includes planning your day instead of having the day plan you.

Procrastination is a dream killer. By taking specific and measurable steps to stop putting off the life you want to live, you can improve your business and relationships and begin to live a life you love. There is an arsenal of tools that can help you in the battle against procrastination. These include wise management of your time, making a plan that allows flexibility for change, and making a commitment to yourself that you want to change the way you handle tasks that you do not enjoy doing.

Start to take control by making a list of the things you need to do. Sort the list by importance. Each day, decide which main item on the list you will do today. Do it first thing the next day. Finish all those little ones in short spurts of time and get them off the list. As you become a "completer," it becomes like a fun game to play. Crossing items off the list gives a lift to your spirit and lets you know you are a winner!

Cynthia Charleen coaches clients to become more productive by clearing the clutter and getting organized. Creating a workable plan for each client is a priority in getting things done. She works as a professional organizer in the Dallas area and is available for consult. You can find out more about what she teaches and does at http://BreakFreeFromClutter.com or you can find her book "Get Your Home Office Organized, Cut the Clutter and Watch Your Productivity Soar" available on Amazon.

Chapter 7
Me and Charlie Brown
by Geoff Hoff

In the musical play called "You're a Good Man, Charlie Brown" based on Charles Schultz' *Peanuts* comic strip, there is a song where all the characters except Snoopy the dog must write a book report on Peter Rabbit. Each kid has his or her own approach to the assignment such as being obsessed with the word count (Lucy), reviewing an entirely different, but more exciting book (Schroeder), and examining the internal philosophic and religious characteristics of the story (Linus). Charlie Brown, of course, gets neurotic and debates with himself on whether or not he should actually start.

His arguments in favor of waiting?

- He's not really rested
- It's not due till Wednesday
- He should be getting fresh air and sunshine
- He works best under pressure

In favor of starting now?

- There'll be lots of pressure if he waits

This is the quintessential procrastinator's lament. It is also how I did my homework through most of my many years of school. I was a lot like old Charlie. It is also how I did much of my work once I entered the work force as an adult. Truth be told, procrastination still takes hold in my life.

Let me say first that there are a lot of differences between being habitually late and procrastinating, although on the surface they may sound the same. I am obsessively on time (or annoyingly early) to business or doctors' appointments, dates with friends, going to a movie or show, etc. And yet, I procrastinate. Somehow, in my fervor-brain, a task is quite distinct from an appointment. With one, I move heaven and earth to getting there. With the other, I find very comfortable and creative ways to avoid getting started. I get more laundry done and have more clean dishes when I need to start a new project than at any other time. (Of course, if the project at hand is doing laundry or dishes, there are many other things I can find for my avoidance strategies.)

But there are things I do when I notice the old pattern of avoiding a task. I share them, not because I think you need to do any of them, but because, in my life, I have found them effective. Let me break them down by some of the strategies I use not to get started and what might be done about each:

I'm Tired

This one seems a no-brainer. Get enough sleep. But what do you do when you already haven't gotten enough sleep? I learned something from my grandmother, who ran the business she and Grandpa owned, took care of the five of us, cooked, cleaned, paid bills, shopped, planned events and carried out those plans, etc., etc. She legitimately got tired a lot. She used to take what she called a "Power Nap." There was a big, over-stuffed chair with a hassock in the corner of the kitchen. She would sit down, put her feet up, close her eyes and snooze. For about ten minutes. Then she'd get up and get back to work, refreshed.

When I first started trying this technique, I would sleep for much more than ten minutes, often as much as a few hours. When waking from such a nap, I would feel sluggish, almost drugged. But when I held it to ten or fifteen minutes (I use an alarm clock, I'm not as disciplined as Grandma, it seems), I would indeed feel refreshed and able to get back to it.

I Haven't Thought About the Task Enough

Often times, a new task requires some creative pre-thought. When you have the luxury of time, you can spend time just cogitating on it, letting your subconscious mind percolate ideas out to your conscious mind. However, when you are in a time crunch with the deadline fast approaching, or the deadline was set very short from the get-go, you must just decide that what's there is enough and sit down and get to work.

At those times, the thought that, "I need to just cogitate" is an indulgence you can't afford. Your task may not come out as brilliantly as it would have with the pre-thought, but you will get it done.

I'm Not Inspired

This is similar to the one above, but there are some differences. We often misinterpret what "inspiration" means and many of us simply will not get started until that vague, ethereal feeling descends upon us. And then, heaven forbid we're doing something noisy or that takes a bit of concentration as our avoidance (can you say Video Games or Netflix?) In those cases, even if you do get "inspired," you won't even notice.

Instead, think of inspiration in a different way: It is simply your subconscious mind feeding you ideas that it generated from all the thoughts you've had to that point. One of the best ways to get inspired is to just get started. Let yourself flounder a bit, let the task be sloppy until the subconscious mind clicks in. And even if it doesn't, you've still gotten started, and, with procrastination, that is usually the highest hurdle.

I Know I can Get It Done in Less Time

This is a real Charlie Brown one. I do it a lot. "Let's see. I said I'd have this done by noon on Wednesday. I know it will take me about an hour and a half to do it. That means I can start at 10 A.M. on Wednesday and still have a half-hour of wiggle room.

But, just like Charlie sings in his song: "Unless something should happen."

And something always happens.

This one is a bit harder to handle. I often don't even realize I haven't given myself enough time until it's too late and I don't have any more time. Because of that, I have to be brutally honest with myself when figuring out when to do things. I have to know my propensity for procrastinating and take that into account. When I'm honest, and that mercurial thing called my mind says, "Aw, hell, you can get that done in a jiffy. Put it off until 10:30. You'll have plenty of time," I have to realize my mind is a liar and plan accordingly. A good rule of thumb is to give myself at least three times as much time as I think I can get it done in. A better rule of thumb is to start the day before I think I have to start. If I get it done sooner, I can do other things. If not, I won't be working under that stressful, beating-heart, sweating pressure that I so seem to thrive on...when my heart can take it.

All of these solutions, of course, are predicated on being honest with yourself. Something old Charlie Brown never quite allowed himself to be.

Geoff Hoff has been a best-selling author of both fiction, how-to and business books. He has also been an actor, an acting teacher, a standup comic and a popular blogger who now teaches creative writing, tech and marketing courses on the Internet. After studying the process of creativity for years, he was amazed to discover that creativity could be practical, it could be taught and it was not only important, but necessary for every entrepreneur. His classes also tend to be a lot of fun. You can find out more about Geoff at http://GeoffHoff.com.

A note from Leslie Cardinal: *Sadly, Geoff Hoff passed away very unexpectedly just a few days after writing this chapter. He was a delightful friend, colleague, and teacher. I'm so glad to be able to include his chapter in this book.*

Chapter 8
Systems for Taking Action
by Gwen Ross

When Leslie approached me about contributing a chapter for a book about procrastination, I'm pretty sure I laughed. I could write about procrastinating, that's for sure! Then she explained that in writing her first book, "I Hate to Be Late!" she had followed a process that helped her transform her ability to be on time. She asked others to share their advice, she tried their advice, and then she also wrote about what she had learned. So I decided to give this approach a try, with the hope that an attempt to improve my own habits would give me insights that could help others as well.

By that point, I had already begun a new habit of striking up conversations with people about efficiency, self-discipline, and procrastination. My previous approaches for trying to improve in these areas had not been as effective as I would have liked. All the techniques I read just went in one ear and out the other as I searched for a *foundation* with which I could understand and apply the techniques effectively.

I began to realize that I could either go on pretending to be perfect, and continue struggling with procrastination as I was; or I could be real, admit to a handful of people that I am not perfect and ask how they do it, and thus open up the possibility of change and improvement that, due to my learning style, the world of books was not opening up to me. So I decided it was worth the risk to admit imperfection and ask about others' experiences and mindsets to find ways I could improve.

As a result, I have had a lot of truly enjoyable conversations, I have received great, foundational advice, and I have discovered that there are many different mindsets and techniques that people use to increase their efficiency and efficacy. If you find yourself frustrated by failed attempts at overcoming procrastination, I suggest talking with efficient people around you to start shifting your mindset. You could hire a consultant or a coach, or bring up the subject with successful colleagues, peers, business owners, or other parents you interact with and admire.

As a result of the conversations I have had and the new approaches I have tried, I discovered two kinds of systems that have helped me make significant progress in overcoming procrastination: creating "triggers" to help me tackle special tasks, and creating routines to help me skim through day-to-day activities.

Triggers

Triggers are events that, consciously or unconsciously, cause us to associate one action with another (for example, coffee upon waking, a drink after work, checking the smart phone between every single activity). Once a habit has formed around a trigger, it can become very strongly engrained. Triggers can also be a powerful tool in habit formation.

I spoke with time management consultant Helene Segura about some of my specific time management issues at home. For example, when my daughter plays by herself after we get home from school, I am in an on-call state of mind waiting for a call to help or play, and this often results in my doing mindless activities so that I can be fully attentive as soon as she calls. Helene suggested that, rather than use her playtime as a trigger to do mindless things, I could use this as a trigger to go through the mail.

This proved helpful, and I modified the approach to tackle some other priorities. I made a "To Do" list on my phone, and used my daughter's playing as a trigger to look at the list and select a task. I discovered I can still be on call and attentive while also working on high priority activities and making the household run more smoothly. And by accomplishing more things while she is playing by herself, I am able to be more present with her at other times.

Transitions

During another conversation, my aunt Debbie gave me her copy of a wonderful book, "It's Hard To Make a Difference When You Can't Find Your Keys" by Marilyn Paul, Ph.D. Keys are one thing I have never had a problem with, but I have struggled with other aspects of organization and punctuality, which the book discusses at length.

The exercises in Paul's book are not of the "go clean out your closet and label your bags keep/toss/donate" variety that we have all read before, but the "look at your habits to see where your hang ups are and what your beliefs are" variety. If you are a strictly practical person, that approach may sound frivolous, but in my experience I have found the end result to be far more effective and lasting than the step-by-step, "practical" books I've read.

In the process of examining my habits, I came to realize that I struggle with transitions. Transitions are periods between activities that can quickly and easily turn to black holes if we are not disciplined about transitioning effectively.

Some people seem to glide with grace and ease from one activity or location to another and never miss a beat.

Other people require more time to transition between activities than others. They need to wrap up loose ends, look around and make sure they have everything, think about where they are going, sit for a minute before they get out of the car, and repeat before moving on to the next activity or location.

I recognize that I am one of those people who generally need time to transition from one activity to another. As I observed this, I wondered how I could use this knowledge to my advantage, and find a way to live more like those who glide with grace and ease between activities. It turns out that it is possible to reduce transitions between activities, with some mindful observation and planning.

Transitions can be harnessed by setting up triggers to group activities together, so that the total number of transitions is reduced, and the efficiency of the transitions is increased. This requires paying close attention to what your transitions are, the activities that need to be done within a time frame, and your personal energy patterns. As a basic example, I will share some activities that I have grouped together to harness my energy and maximize the efficiency of a daily transition.

After Dinner Transition

I am a morning person, so I have noticed that after dinner when my stomach is full and energy levels wane, transitions can take twice as long as I approach bedtime. If I could accomplish the after dinner activities more easily or with more energy, I could get them done more quickly and therefore get to bed earlier, and have more energy the next day. So I decided to focus on the after dinner transition.

If I get bogged down in each step or get sidetracked by unnecessary activities, then there is a cumbersome and arduous transition between activities. But by grouping activities together, I do not allow myself a transition at all - each activity is a trigger to move on the next. As soon as I get up from the table, I feed the dog, clear the table, take vitamins, put away leftovers, clean up the dishes, brush my teeth, and wash my face. I do not stop - I skim across the top.

I know my energy is relatively low at this late time of day. So I realize that sitting down at any point during this part of the process would introduce an unnecessary transition. This would ultimately either make it take longer to get to bed, or cause me to procrastinate on cleaning up all the way, which would make supper start later the next day. Instead, with the streamlined grouping of activities, the critical path to bedtime is simplified.

You may be thinking to yourself, "Congratulations, you have discovered what is called a routine. This is how the rest of the world already operates." And...you are probably right. I have always read that routines are important, but I had yet to come across a compelling description of why they are important and how to form one.

When I envisioned a routine as a grouping of activities in order to reduce the feeling and duration of transition between them, the importance became obvious to me. It made sense as to how I might go about constructing routines for myself. Routines that are intentional and deliberate can be used both to prevent procrastination on daily tasks, and to complete daily tasks more efficiently in order to make time for more projects.

Find What Works For You

When dealing with procrastination in yourself and others, keep in mind that different mindsets and techniques resonate with different people. Some techniques may be effective for those around you, and will not resonate with you at all, and vice versa. Keep searching and experimenting until you find a mindset, technique, or resource that works for you. If I could improve, I know you can, too.

Gwen Ross is a software developer. She enjoys reading, talking, and writing about personal development. If you have benefited from what she has learned about procrastination, she would love to hear from you at gwenyross@gmail.com.

Chapter 9
Break the Procrastination Habit

by Kit Rosato

You have heard it said and you know it is true, we all have only 24 hours a day...no one gets more or less. So what is the big difference between those who are most productive and stay on task and those of us who are procrastinators? The most productive people use their time to great advantage. Procrastinators waste more time than others.

Are you a time waster? Time wasters over think, plan too long, seek perfection and struggle with imagined fears of how something will turn out. I still struggle with this in some areas of my life. The first step is to admit you are probably doing some things wrong. What a relief to just admit it! This is the first step in breaking the procrastination habit. Once identified, you can change the behaviors that aren't serving you.

Everyone deals with procrastination and the temptation to put off boring, challenging and fearful tasks or projects. There is no 100% cure. You can, however, break the grip this habit has over your life that is keeping you from achieving your goals and becoming the person you were meant to be. The struggle may not go away permanently, but you will gain control to the extent it doesn't rule your life. Progress is the goal, not perfection.

Three areas that I have focused on to tame this beast and set me up for success are the following:

- Mental Discipline
- Setting the Stage
- Attitude of Gratitude and Enthusiasm

Mental Discipline

Conquering your procrastination habit begins not with taking physical action steps first, but in your mind. You are taking action steps every day but it's the wrong actions if your thoughts aren't aligned first. Most people persist in the habit because of a failure to commit to change the behavior. There is a big difference in the attitude of "I will try to improve and see what happens" verses the attitude "I am going to stop procrastination dead in its tracks and learn the necessary strategies to help me change this destructive habit."

Getting clear and committed on the desire to change and discovering your "big why" that motivates you is very important. Your "big why" is not the pursuit of a money goal, as some people think. That won't see you through the tough times and procrastination hurdles. What you need to nail down is who you want to serve. What will your success enable you to do that will bring joy and fulfillment to your life and others?

This step of developing the mental discipline may be the hardest. You need to spend some time in reflection and examining why and when you procrastinate. What sets off the cycle for you? Is the task or project in line with your "big why"? Which tasks do you put off? How do you feel at the time and what behaviors do you substitute for the task that needs to get done?

When the urge to procrastinate grabs you do you jump on Facebook or Twitter, or take an unnecessary break, or tell yourself you will get to it after a few more minutes doing something else? Identify your avoidance behaviors so you can recognize them when they start to happen, stop yourself, and mentally redirect yourself to the task you need to do. It might be helpful to make a list so you can review it and become more familiar with the ways you procrastinate. An online tool I have been using is called Rescue Time. It sends you a weekly report of where you spend your time online and helps you identify time wasters.

The other part of mental discipline is positive self-talk and visualizing yourself accomplishing the task and feeling great at the same time. Self-talk is a powerful way to mentally get you in the frame of mind to delve into your to-do list. Next is visualization. They go hand in hand.

Some people are great at visualization and find it easy to do. I find it easy in certain areas of my life and a struggle in others. It really is important that your positive affirmations line up with how you visualize the task or achieving the goal. Telling yourself you don't procrastinate any more but mentally seeing yourself as rushing at the last minute to accomplish something is incongruent. The two need to match to break the habit.

This is a very powerful technique! Trying to knuckle down and attack a project or task with sheer willpower often doesn't work. That can feel like a huge struggle and can loop you back into the same pattern of procrastination, dreading the work that needs to be done. Until I started using both self-talk and visualization I felt like the character in the movie "Groundhog Day", repeating the same behaviors over and over until I figured it out.

Setting the Stage

OK, you got past the hard part. This is the fun step of organizing your work space so you are the most productive. For some people it is their well- organized desk at home or clean office space and surrounding cabinets. For others, a comfy chair in a secluded area works best. I know people who like to retreat to a coffee shop with their laptop and head phones. If you work in a cubical or office somewhere it may entail setting the stage with pictures and quotes and other things that inspire you to stay on task.

I start my mornings in our sunroom with a steaming cup of fresh coffee, a comfy blanket, legal pads, and the quiet and stillness of early morning before anyone else is awake. Your best time to tackle your work may be evenings. You get to choose. Just make it as welcoming as you can. If you prefer a messy space but you are capable of finding whatever you need that is ok too.

What all the setting choices have in common is a way to eliminate distractions, such as using head phones or having a sign posted that you are not to be disturbed. Don't be afraid to set boundaries with people tempted to interrupt you. Closed doors, set working times, or perhaps a special hat on your head that even the youngest of family members can recognize as a do not disturb sign, can work.

Also, be sure to turn off devices you are not using and have all the notes, tools and supplies at hand. When you have set a stage that is inviting you will feel good about getting to work instead of procrastinating. You are aiming for the best work environment for you, not someone else. There is no need to let someone else dictate this important choice. Even in the most challenging situations you can carve out time and space to get things done in a timely manner.

Attitude of Gratitude and Enthusiasm

Your mindset is now geared for success, your work space is set for productivity, and all that is left is to start your day with the right attitude. Being grateful for all the things you have, and the incredible privilege of a brand new day with 24 hours to work towards your dreams and goals, is a gift. Having a gratitude journal may help you get your attitude in the right place. It is impossible to feel thankful and fearful at the same time. Try it! I consider my gratitude journal essential to my success.

Most super productive people who have broken the habits of procrastination bring the right attitude and enthusiasm to the work they do and have eliminated their time wasters to a large extent. They see time as their friend and as a gift to accomplish all the great things they want to do. With the right attitude you will start viewing the unappealing, boring, "have-to" tasks as challenges that will make you stronger and more self- confident in the process.

With the right attitude your self-discipline increases and your "can do" spirit takes center stage. You become excited to create your "to-do" lists, prioritize your tasks, eliminate your time wasters, and create a schedule that works for you. You easily incorporate the time saving tactics you like that fit into the life you are designing.

For example, if your doctor is running late you no longer are annoyed. You see it as a chance to whip out your notepad or phone and start planning your next project or perhaps writing, creating a new list, making an outline, etc.

With the right attitude you will find yourself accomplishing so much more! You will even begin to notice how other people complain and make excuses for procrastination. Now you are capable of catching yourself when you fall into this trap and can be an encouragement to others.

In Conclusion

I hope that some of what I have shared here will be helpful to you in breaking your procrastination habit. Until I created the right mindset, a welcoming work space, and the proper attitude, I found myself in the constant struggle to change this habit. Today I am on a better path to slaying this beast. I wish the same for you!

Kit Rosato is passionate about learning, growing her online marketing business, sharing and inspiring others to do the same. She loves selling on Amazon and marketing in different niches. You can follow her journey and connect with her at http://KitRosato.com.

Chapter 10
Procrastinating in Italian
by Maria Lassila

I remember one of my proudest moments at a job I once had. Someone in the office referred to me as "the girl who gets things done." I must admit that I considered myself very productive, so it was rather gratifying to hear that others felt the same way.

I was working for a company that made luxury golf clothing and all of our production was in Italy. I was based in the corporate headquarters in southern California and one of my main responsibilities was to make sure that the polo shirts, sweater vests, and trousers that made up each season's collection were made according to our instructions and shipped on time to our warehouse.

While I traveled to Milan a couple of times a year to make the rounds of the various factories we contracted with, I mainly worked from our office via phone and fax with our agent who was based in northern Italy. She and I worked well together. She was Italian and had worked with our factory partners for many years both for our company and for her other clients. She was used to our "American" way of working: the deadline is the deadline and once it's set, it is no longer open for discussion.

I was accustomed to her style as well. She would regale me with the excuses from our suppliers as to why they were not going to deliver on time. I would listen to her stories and then wait patiently for her to finish with how, in the end, she had (usually) managed to convince them to honor their commitments. A combination of threats, pleas and creative ways around the obstacles seemed to be the way she got things done.

Fast forward a couple of years and I was now the one living in Milan, sent there to open our Italian office and to replace our agent who had decided to retire. Now I was the one on the front line with the factories – listening to all of the reasons why they wouldn't be able to respect the delivery agreements that we'd defined only a couple of months prior.

The Italian outlook on procrastination is that it is a fact of life. Other things come up that need to be attended to. The original deadline was not realistic and surely cannot be expected to be met. Oh, you really meant it? It's truly a problem if it's late?

When this happens, superhero measures are then instituted, with everyone in the building pitching in to make it happen and seal the tape on the carton 30 seconds prior to the last minute before it is scheduled to be picked up. Or maybe a few minutes of distracting the courier with small talk and an offer of coffee are necessary to gain the last little bit of time needed to finish.

Then, once the impossible has been achieved, of course it's necessary to celebrate the heroism of everyone who contributed to fending off the disaster of not meeting the deadline. To relive the brilliance and cunning of overcoming the obstacles and crossing the finish line victoriously.

At first, this ritual of Italian life pushed me toward developing an ulcer. It always looked like they'd never make it, and in fact they sometimes didn't. Over time, I became accustomed to it--almost. And little by little, as the years went by, I began to adopt procrastination as a way of life myself.

I've now lived in Milan for over 15 years. A few years ago I took stock of myself and my situation and realized that while many of the Italian habits that I'd adopted – eating well, for example – were positive additions to my life, the habit of procrastination most decidedly was not. Especially once I left the world of employment behind and became my own boss as an entrepreneur.

Somehow it's easy to forgive yourself for not finishing exactly when you promised yourself you would. Somehow it's reasonable to accept your own excuses why something's not quite on time. Nobody is going to hold you accountable for the missed deadline which, after all, you set yourself and probably somewhat arbitrarily, when all is said and done. You certainly have good reasons why you didn't accomplish what you'd set out to, and you'll certainly get it done very shortly. You are sure of it.

Fairly quickly I recognized that I was going to have to rid myself of this unwelcome habit if I were going to be successful. Many were the days that I started off with good intentions, to-do list in hand in the early morning hours, full of energy and drive, looking forward to crossing off items one by one. But few were the days when I managed to mark off the most important, when I managed to slay the fiercest dragons that I'd set my sights on.

Distractions seemed to crop up everywhere. Some were "important" – such as administrative details that were boring yet vital. Others were just more attractive – closely monitoring email accounts for new arrivals, checking social media accounts "just for 2 minutes," or rearranging and tidying up my office. The days drew to a close without anything meaningful having been accomplished. My trusty to-do list had only the easiest and least important – read least lucrative – tasks marked as complete.

I had to understand what was happening. How did all of the hours drain away with hardly anything to show for them? I'd been at my desk for a good part of the day, yet I couldn't recall precisely what I'd managed to complete. I'd gone out on various errands, but somehow the time used up didn't correspond to the end results.

My solution was to get myself a notebook and to browbeat myself into recording every single thing that I did. My idea was that if it worked for dieters trying to understand exactly what they ate and spenders determined to know where there income was disappearing to, it could work for me in understanding where I was investing my time.

So I kept track, asking what I was actually doing. Opening up Facebook to see how the rest of the world was killing time? Getting up to browse the contents of the kitchen well before lunchtime? Chatting on social phone calls with people I didn't really need to catch up with? Reading through sales letters showing up in my inbox for things I probably had no use for?

I forced myself to note each and every thing that I devoted a piece of my workday to - along with the beginning and end times - so I'd be able to calculate how much of my day I could actually justify to my new boss, the non-procrastinating me. And I became painfully aware of how much of my time was being used up by things that were perhaps instantly gratifying, but not useful in moving me closer to my goals.

They say knowledge is power. I can certainly vouch that it is difficult to argue with. Once I had the hard proof, gathered by my own hand, of where I was allowing myself to allocate my time, there was no one to blame but myself. Becoming aware and forcing myself to examine my actions – or lack of them – was the catalyst to making myself finally a bit less Italian and much less of a procrastinator. And to reinvent myself into my previous productive self – the person who gets things done.

Maria Lassila has been living in Milan, Italy for over 15 years, since her transplant from the west coast of the U.S. After years of addiction to the apparel industry, she now helps small businesses and professionals show up where their potential clients are searching for them online. She works with both the English-speaking community in Milan as well as US-based companies, including her family's movie theater business in eastern Washington State. Connect with Maria at http://AnAmericanInMilan.com.

Chapter 11
Procrastination – the "Good" Habit

by Nita Bauer

Wasn't it amazing when we learned that chocolate is good for us, that drinking wine actually has a health benefit? What if we found out all our bad habits are good for us, too, even procrastination? Wouldn't that be the ideal world?

I love the idea that the Latin meaning of "procrastinate" has a power statement built into it:

The prefix *pro-* means "forward."

The adjective *crastinus* means "tomorrow."

You might need to drink a glass of wine to see it, but doesn't "pro" imply intentional, and "tomorrow" have a future based connotation to it? It's almost like: *I see what needs to be done, and I am intentionally delaying action to serve my objectives.* Tell me that doesn't have "good" written all over it! I can feel my head rise with pride as I write it.

So, if there really is an intended purpose in delaying action that serves us, what would it be?

Fire

My friend, Mark, likes to wait until the last minute because, he says, the less time he has to do something the quicker he can get it done. He calls it "lighting a fire under his caboose." I wouldn't say he's an adrenalin junkie—though he did break a leg skydiving—but it sounds like he's trying to build up enough steam to push himself across the deadline. I know when my guests are on their way, I can clean house pretty darned fast. And when I only have an hour to work on my novel, I can be focused and intentional. So compressing the window of opportunity to get something done does have its advantages. That's good, isn't it?

Ice

My husband, on the other hand, likes to postpone his projects until the adrenalin rush cools. I think he gets overwhelmed when he looks at a project that's too big—like cleaning the garage. Fight or flight takes over, and waiting lets the stress level dissipate. Some might say, "Come on, honey, this cooldown has turned into an ice age," but I can certainly relate to the intended purpose. I know when my boss asks for something I've never done before, my brain starts racing like a train about to go off its rails. That's when I need a chill-pill. After a fifteen minute diversion, the engine cools down, and I can deal with the task more rationally. Cooling off makes good sense, right?

Universal Timing

My friend, Rich, has a theory that our lives are governed by a divine energy that moves us to act at the exact right time. Waiting for the train to arrive, so to speak, we seem to be in a state of inaction. But he says we're actually operating in alignment with our life's purpose. You simply cannot get on the train until it arrives. Personally, I can list several times in my past that felt like I was waiting too long. Then, there was a precise moment when I absolutely knew what I needed to do. Major life decisions happened in a split second. I jumped on the train, and away I went—just like I planned it that way. What could be better than that?

Prioritization

As for me, I often find myself at the ticket counter, looking at all my options. The want-to-dos are always competing with the have-to-dos for position on my list. Of course, even if I wanted to do everything, there isn't enough time or resources for all of it. Some days I just throw my hands up in frustration. On good days, I can rack and stack everything on the list according to its value or importance. Things that don't make the cut simply get pushed off until they become more urgent. If I work the list right, I can make most of the stops I need to make and end up at home just in time for the next episode of "Scandal." Is it procrastinating if I save the dishes for later? I say "no," I'm prioritizing.

"Everything in moderation;" isn't that what they always say? First they give us a bar of chocolate and tell us it's good for us. Then they tape a disclaimer to the bottom of it. Yep! I'm afraid this "Procrastination is good for you" ideology has a disclaimer, too: *Your Life Conductor has determined that persistently waiting until the last minute, letting things cool off too long, waiting indefinitely for the exact right second, or always shuffling things to the bottom of the list may be hazardous to your future.*

I don't know about you, but I figured that out the same way I figured out about chocolate and wine—experience. Procrastination, in the right hands, might be a surgeon's scalpel or an artist's brush, but in mine it's a shovel on a mound of M&Ms. So how can we pull this off? I mean, if we really want to make procrastination work for us instead of against us, what's the next step? Here are a couple of suggestions to get your ideas rolling.

Light your own fire

If you're someone who likes a little stress to push you across the finish line, then use that to your advantage. Make your own deadlines. Break your primary task into smaller blocks of work with your own by-when dates and a promise to stick to them. If you really need someone to hold your feet to the fire, ask a trusted partner to routinely follow up on your progress. I recommend you don't use your spouse for this. Trust me; that has a completely different kind of stress.

Refrigerate, don't freeze

If you find a task so overwhelming you want to put it in the freezer and forget about it, consider using the refrigerator instead. Give your cool down an expiration date. Of course, that means that you have to be rational about how long is reasonable. Think milk, and don't give yourself permission to grow science projects. Then, organize tasks for your project into smaller subsets that use the same resources or need to be handled on the same schedule.

Compartmentalizing this way makes the whole project less overwhelming. Finally, keep things fresh by rotating the chill period with some real action. We've used this technique at home to get the chores done on the weekend by rotating speed-cleaning during commercials with our TV viewing. It works, and it adds in a little fun at the same time. "Hold on, Olivia. I'm still vacuuming."

Turn timing into an Art

There are amazing moments when waiting for exactly the right second adds an edge of crispness to perfection. There's the runner who conserves her energy for the last sprint, the obstetrician who knows when it's time to push, and the stock trader who uses waiting to enhance her portfolio. Unfortunately, that kind of timing only comes after diligent training and practice. If you want to give yourself the advantage of Universal Timing, become the expert at what you're doing. Learn the science behind it, and then experiment with your timing until your precision feels like art. That way you'll know when the train is coming long before it arrives.

Make a Map

Yes, prioritizing is a purposeful way to make sure the most important things on the list get done. If you're like me, though, there's at least one thing that always get shuffled to the bottom of the list—like going to the gym. Another way to work efficiently is to organize things according to where the task is performed. If I map my daily travels, it's clear that the gym-stop should occur either before or after work, not after I get home— where "Scandal" is already waiting. Switching from list view to map view, I can see where to fit it in and still be mindful of priorities. Besides, I know how to use the DVR.

Personally, I think procrastination, like chocolate, got a bad rap. It's only bad for you when you over-indulge. So the next time you're racing around trying to get something done at the last minute, staring at an insurmountable project, or trying to decide when or if something will ever get done, ask yourself, "How can I use the power of procrastination to get through this?" Then light a fire in the fireplace and map your way over to the fridge for a bottle of wine. By now, we've turned timing into an art. I've already got the chocolate, and "Scandal" starts in five minutes. The dishes can wait for a commercial.

Nita Bauer is an Information Technology professional, author, and life coach. Follow her blog at www.NitaBauer.com .

Chapter 12
One Day, When My To-Do List Is Empty...

Or, Making Time for Our Important Work Amid the Demands of a Full Life

by Steve Arensberg

A while ago, I had an afternoon miraculously open up in my otherwise packed schedule. No driving my son around, no work to finish up. I now had time I could spend on just about anything I wanted. This would be several hours of uninterrupted creative time, perfect for getting some solid writing done. Awesome, I thought. Let's do this!

So what did I do? I painted the dining room.

That's right. Instead of spending time on my own projects, I picked the next item on my to-do list, and did that instead. The dining room needed done, I told myself. It's next on the schedule. It hasn't been painted in a while, and needs it. It's one of the few rooms left in the house to be painted, and then it will be done.

All good reasons. But I often seem to have "good reasons" for doing something else instead of spending time on my writing.

I find myself doing this rather often: focusing on the things that *must* be done, rather than on the things that *should* be done, particularly those things that support my creating art and putting it out into the world. And that act of creation and sharing is both a tremendous gift and an awesome responsibility, no matter who we are, and no matter what our individual art is.

So how do we balance the "must be done" with the "should be done"? How do we stop procrastinating on those things that are important to our art, by doing other important things, for other people? When is it our time, and our art's time?

The Four Quadrants

In *The Seven Habits of Highly Effective People*, Stephen Covey talks about the time management grid, in which he divides time into four quadrants based on two criteria: urgency and importance. He further states that the **Important Not Urgent** (INU) tasks are the key things that allow us to most grow as people. It is tasks like strategy, planning, relationship-building, exercise, and all those other "know we should do but can't find the time because of all the 'must do now' things taking up our days" kind of tasks.

INU is where my personal projects live, as well. Things like my blog, and writing, and exercise, and meditation. Those things that allow me to be my best, to do my best work, to rejuvenate myself, to rest and recover, to be a better person.

And yet hungry urgent tasks, like driving teenagers to their many activities, work deadlines, laundry, grocery shopping, and all the miscellaneous emergencies (important or not) seem to take up most of my time.

Scheduling INU Projects

I find the "four quadrants" model the most powerful and memorable idea from the book. Covey spends more time describing how to make more time for INU activities (defining roles, selecting goals, and scheduling). The first two I find less helpful, but the scheduling phase is VERY important, and is the only way I seem to get those INU things done.

A to-do list is a great tool, but it keeps us focused on urgency and less on importance. I've found that when managed with a to-do list, my INU activities keep getting pushed down and carried over, bullied by the rush of new urgent tasks.

Scheduling, on the other hand, works really well for INU activities. Blocking off time on my calendar (for me, particularly in the early morning hours) gives me the time to pursue those INU objectives. Each week, I endeavor to set aside those blocks of time to work on my projects.

The challenge is saying "no" to other activities that might usurp that INU time. And that requires more than blocking the time on the calendar. It requires understanding the reasons we let other things take precedence in our lives, over those things that are important to us. In other words, understanding the reasons that trigger us to procrastinate.

Procrastination Triggers

In my experience, the three triggers that most often cause me to procrastinate are: perfectionism, obligation, and fear. I imagine most of you reading this book procrastinate because of at least one of those same triggers, if not all three! And you probably have a few interesting procrastination triggers of your own.

Perfectionism

Perfectionism is the easiest to identify. Raised as a dutiful student of standard education, getting "them all right" was the order of the day, and that desire to get a perfect score was ingrained in me from an early age. In my adult life I added "editor" to my list of character traits (and resume), which further solidified the desire for anything I did to be "error free"—perfect.

The conflict is that we as humans are fallible. We make mistakes. We aren't perfect. But when we put something out into the world—when we create art—we expect it to be perfect. We **want** to deliver perfection, rather than simply "our best work" (whatever that is at the moment), and so we either: don't create, or we create but don't share with the world.

Obligation

Obligation is the word I use to describe both the need to do something for someone else in order to feel validated, and the guilt we feel when we do something for ourselves, instead of using that time to serve someone else.

I'm reminded of a Q&A for a workshop I attended a few years ago, and one of my fellow students was struggling to figure out how to get her "yoga salon" to the next level, serving young mothers in need of exercise and pampering and self-care. And the key problem she was facing was that these mothers felt guilty because when they took care of themselves, they were taking time away from their children.

The simple math of this statement is true. Spending one hour a day to exercise and sip a mocha and get a hot-stones massage takes that hour away from time that could be spent with one's children. But this is not a simple, one-for-one trade. When we give time to things which build us up, the quality of the time we can offer to those important people in our lives is exponentially greater that in it is when we don't practice self-care (including doing our art).

I'm guilty of this one, too—particularly when it comes to family. You'll do all sorts of unreasonable things to support your spouse or kids, but you refuse to do those same sorts of things for yourself, or let anybody else do that for you.

And in doing so, we limit the joy we have in life, our personal growth, and our impact on the world. If we are constantly doing for others, we have no time or energy to do for ourselves. Our time and energy is limited, and what we put out into the world is likewise limited.

Fear

Fear is the third, and most powerful reason I procrastinate. It's the main reason, more than the other reasons combined, that I procrastinate.

The primary fear that fuels my procrastination is fear of being vulnerable, of showing "the real me" as represented by my work, and being judged and found unworthy. Over time I've come to realize that my perfectionism is a mask that covers that fear of rejection, because the rejection is not just of my creation, but it's a rejection of **me**—of my essential self. If I put out my best, most personal, most true to myself work, and it's rejected... then so am I.

That sort of fear can be paralyzing. And it kept me frozen for many years, afraid to create and looking for any excuse to keep that work at a distance. Or creating for myself, but never putting anything into the world. Fighting procrastination on both sides of the "make art" coin: the creation itself, and sharing that art with the world.

One of my favorite books about this struggle is Steven Pressfield's, *The War of Art*. Pressfield calls this fear, this procrastination, this thing that keeps us from making our art **Resistance**. And he says we must battle it every day.

So how do we do that?

Tactics for Defeating Procrastination

Nike's slogan "Just Do It" is great advertising, but it's not particularly helpful as a tactic for overcoming procrastination, particularly the procrastination that grows from a powerful emotional or historical place in our lives. It might work when battling the procrastination "minions"—the simple tasks that just need an extra push for us to get them done. But for those big "boss" triggers, like Perfectionism, Obligation, Fear? Those require stronger tactics to defeat.

The following are tactics I've adopted that help me overcome my three boss triggers; I hope they will help you against yours as well.

First, for Perfectionism, my preferred (and most successful) tactic is **Practice**. When I'm preparing to sit down and write something, I tell myself "This is practice." Even my daily journaling now is called "Writing Practice" (or WP for short, with the date). And that's exactly what it is. Calling it practice helps take the pressure off. There's no expectation of delivering some perfect result.

Easier said than done, you say? Try it. Turn "making your art" into "art practice" and call it that out loud. Put that name in your appointment you scheduled for it (you did, schedule it, right?). Say to yourself as you start (always the most challenging time) "I'm just practicing." Remind yourself that practice is about trying things, experimenting, learning. It's **not** about what you produce. It's about what you do, and do consistently.

Second, when fighting Obligation, my most useful tactic is **Accountability**. Obligation is for me about consistently putting the needs of others ahead of my own. I imagine a number of you are similar in this. It's so much easier to do for others than to think about "selfishly" taking time for ourselves and our needs.

Accountability is a great way to trick our need to oblige others into serving those things that support us. I've been able to set up others in my life to serve as accountability partners—those who will hold me accountable to what I promise to myself (because, in effect, I'm promising it to them).

For writing, it's having a regular writing partner, James, with whom I meet and share a Saturday afternoon "banging the keys" at a favorite local haunt. The promise of getting together once or twice a month, and being together, keeps us both producing the writing. (It's how I'm writing this chapter...)

For health, it's hiring a fitness coach to help me design a plan for nutrition and exercise. But more importantly, it's the daily check-ins, and my desire not to let him down, that keep me sticking to the program.

Finally, facing Fear, my particular Fear, is like facing the end-of-game boss in a video game. He's big—not so much in size, but in his power to disrupt me and keep me from doing what I'm on the planet to do. And that's exactly his role.

I use a pair of tactics to get me through. The first is **mindfulness meditation**, which helps me to be aware of my thoughts and emotions, and to observe them from a place of distance and kindness. This helps me identify times when Fear is influencing my actions.

The second tactic is **self-love**. This is treating myself the same way I would treat a dear friend—with kindness and empathy, and with genuine affection and liking for the person I am today. Counseling and coaching has helped tremendously as I've struggled to learn this. Another option (less expensive than counseling and/or coaching) that I've found is the book *Love Yourself Like Your Life Depends on It*, by Kamal Ravikant.

These tactics, both identifying and scheduling time for INU activities, and identifying and battling procrastination triggers, continue to help me make positive changes in my life, even in the face of Resistance. I hope that these ideas will help you overcome your own procrastination, and find and do great work in the world (instead of painting your dining room).

Steve Arensberg writes at the intersection of story, inspiration, and self-improvement. His blog, www.freeofgravity.com offers aspiring heroes help revealing their origin stories and increasing self-knowledge, defining their purpose, and creating habit and practices to build their heroic self.

Chapter 13
How I Beat Procrastination and Got My Life Moving Again

by Steve Matuszak

Do you feel like you're stuck? Is there something piled up that you just can't seem to tackle, no matter how hard you try?

That's what happened to me some years ago. Mine was a pile of paper, memos, and documents that literally loomed like a mountain. No matter what I tried, I just couldn't get going on taking action and making decisions on what those documents represented.

But heaven smiled down at me and help came from an unexpected source. I discovered a solution. It was simple. It worked. It solved my problem then and many times later whenever I needed to apply it. Best of all, it works for others too when I teach them this solution.

I'm not exactly sure why the solution works. It just seems to turn on a switch that allows us to take action in a way we couldn't before.

Here is what happened to me. I was a young Senior VP in a relatively large banking organization in New York. Several important departments reported to me and my management duties took a lot of time and energy.

Suddenly, out of the blue, I started running a low grade fever and became weaker and weaker. I had so little energy that I could spend only a few hours a day at my desk. My doctor prescribed several tests but none of them showed the cause of my condition. He and his associates were stumped.

The result of this had a very adverse impact on my work habits, as you can imagine. I found where in the past I would look at a communication and make a quick phone call or decision right on the spot, I now I found myself saying "I can't do that right now. I'll do it tomorrow."

That is where the habit of procrastination began in my life.

I'm happy to tell you that after several weeks more of medical testing and some time spent in the hospital for observation, the doctors found I had contracted amoebic dysentery which was zapping all of my strength. That was quickly dealt with and I was back on my feet almost overnight.

My secretary retrieved the stack of communications that had accumulated during the illness. I started reviewing them and was able to make the decisions necessary to get the day to day activities in my Division moving again.

The stack of many of the accumulated documents was still there, however. By and large they represented longer range issues like planning and goal setting. I found myself so busy with the here and now that I was neglecting getting into those time consuming issues.

The demon of procrastination was at work. A habit had formed. I found myself saying "I can get to that later" but I never did. Something drastic needed to be done, but I didn't know what. Fortunately that something turned out to come from a kindly gentleman who loved to mentor younger executives. I was studying his course on how to become a more effective manager.

He gave a couple of suggestions in the course that really resonated with me. I had a flash insight on how I might apply them to my procrastination situation and suddenly everything "clicked." I quickly put those insights to work and suddenly found I was able to tackle the momentous mountain I had been avoiding. Amazingly, once I got to work on it, it was done in less than a day!

Here is what I did. First I found a day in my calendar where I could set aside the full day to work only on this task. Then I sat down and looked at what needed to be done and made a conscious decision to devote that ONE day to going all-out on cleaning up the accumulation. I put that statement of determination in writing of a piece of paper.

Then, on the evening before the designated day, I mapped out how I was going to proceed. I put that in writing too.

Early the next morning my secretary and I got started. I reviewed the plan of the night before and proceeded step by step on what to do with each accumulated document. Decisions were made on each, as to whether to delegate to the departments heads, to conduct further research, or to put it on the calendar for focused attention at another time.

I was astounded to find we were done by early afternoon. We had completed reviewing and taking action on every document and every task in the large accumulation. The mountain was gone! That was a major lesson for me. Ever since then I have used those techniques on any task or project I am tempted to put off to another day.

Here is a quick summary of the steps I follow:

- Take any task or project you have allowed to accumulate and determine you are going to devote one day to going all-out to clean it up once and for all.
- Put that appointment on your calendar.

- Write out on paper (important) a statement of your determination to go all-out on cleaning up the task or project.
- Write down on paper what needs to be done on this project (the nature of what you have been avoiding). Let it percolate in your mind the next few hours or days.
- The night before, map out a plan for what needs to be done, and how, as you go all-out tomorrow on cleaning it up.
- Early the next morning, first thing before anything else, implement your plan.
- Bask in the joy of completing the task.

NOTE: it is important to write out your determination and plans the old fashioned way – with pen and paper. Not on an electronic device. There is something about your brain connecting as you write it out that gives the power to these steps.

Go ahead now and give it a try. It works for me and also for those to whom I've revealed the steps. If you do try it let me know how it worked out. I will be grateful. Thanks and much success.

Steve Matuszak has retired from many successful careers and now, among other endeavors, devotes his time to advising those who are "stuck" in some area of their life. He teaches quick solutions he calls Success Hacks™ which break his students free to achieve more success in their personal lives and careers. You can learn more about Steve's solutions and how they can help you break free and have more success too at www.QuickSuccessHacks.com

Chapter 14
The Law of Attraction and Procrastination

by Sue Ascioti-Plange

When most of us think about how to avoid procrastination and the low or depressed feelings that come with it, our thoughts automatically go to the negative. We have thoughts such as "If I can just beat or defeat procrastination in my life, my life will be great!" Procrastination does keep us from living our best lives. But why do we procrastinate, especially when we can clearly see how wonderful our lives would be if we didn't?

There are many reasons for procrastination. These can include indecision, stress, fatigue, depression, feeling as though we do not have enough information to succeed, disorganization, fear of failure, and even fear of success. You can't move though procrastination overnight. If you are a procrastinator, you have been accumulating these habits over a lifetime. But you can move through procrastination by making a disciplined effort to get at the roots of the problem.

Until I was in sixth grade, I was the ultimate procrastinator when it came to homework. I would put it off and put it off, making every excuse from being exhausted to, "I didn't even understand the assignment." One evening, at around 8:30 my dad came into my bedroom. I can *still* picture the corner desk in my room, the pictures on the walls, the window being open, and me being in bed. He asked if I had completed my report on Christopher Columbus. I said no, adding that I would get up early in the morning and do it because it was due the next day. My dad made me get out of bed, sit at my desk and work on that report all night long!

My dad was my first accountability partner. He taught me that if I faced the issue head on I could move through it. I completed the assignment and turned it in the next morning. This experience was life changing for me and I think of it each time I have something big I need to move through.

When it comes to procrastination, all achievements should be rewarded. I have been looking at one particular drawer that I have wanted to clean out for months now. This week I got it done and gave myself the praise I deserved for this. Yes, it was not organizing my entire house, yet it was most definitely praiseworthy!

Here are some tips for moving through procrastination:

1. Take full responsibility for all aspects of your life. One of the main causes of procrastination is the habit many people have of blaming their lack of success on circumstances. When you tell yourself that failures are caused by circumstances beyond your control, you are preparing yourself for a lifetime of procrastination.

    A very important distinction is the difference between "blame" and "responsibility." When reading "Take full responsibility for all aspects of your life" your first thought might be "I am not responsible for my procrastination because I learned it from my mom. I never saw her get anything done on time." Your tendency may be to blame her for your procrastination and the fact that you are not meeting your life goals. When you are in blame, you are in a negative state, and if you are like the majority of us, this will increase negative experiences. On the other hand, when you take responsibility for something, you acknowledge that you are in control of your life circumstances, even if they have not been ideal. You eliminate the sense of being a victim. You are in a proactive, positive state. You learn from what has taken place and you express gratitude for all of your experiences because each one, even the ones you have experienced as not so good, will lead you to toward a better life. You are taking measures to "course correct." You are in a state of humility, openness and positivity.

2. Just do it. Successful people know that their success depends on a commitment to do whatever it takes to reach a goal. Success in all projects, large and small, is determined by the actions you take and your ability to stay focused on your goals. This is true whether your goal is to reduce clutter at home, lose weight, restore a relationship, or complete a major project at work. Projects come in all different shapes, sizes, and levels of importance, but the principles that determine their success or failure are always the same: focus, determination, self-discipline, and confidence. What can you do this week so that you can say "I did it!" and feel the excitement of accomplishment?

3. Establish your priorities. What does it mean to change so that you can reprioritize? To change is to

choose a behavior different from the one you're using now. We all have to fight the drift toward procrastination every day. If are not taking positive actions toward your goals, you need to get your priorities right. Make a list of your priorities at work, at home, for your personal health, growth and in your relationships.

4. Make a commitment to make something happen in at least one of your high-priority items every day. William James said "Nothing is so fatiguing as the eternal hanging on of an uncompleted task." Think of the mental energy that will be relieved and that can be focused on your life goals when your daunting "to do list" containing the same items each and every day is no longer always full of the same tasks!

5. Focus on the result you want to achieve. The more you focus on problems, the more discouraged you're likely to feel and the more the problems will show up in your life. If you are not getting what you want out of life, you probably suffer from a lack of focus. How can you change your focus? One way is to eliminate negative words and phrases from your vocabulary. Some examples of these are "no, not, can't, I don't know." You will be amazed at how your life will change by implementing this step.

6. Give your full attention to whatever you're doing. When you concentrate on the things that can go wrong, you can't stay focused on the job you're doing. Failure is the inevitable consequence of a lack of focus; if I think I'm going to do a bad job, I probably will, or I may never even get started on it at all.

7. Set up a reward system for yourself. There are a few television shows that I enjoy watching. The system I have set up is that I record these shows and watch them while on the elliptical trainer at the gym. I won't allow myself to watch them at home. Instead, I reward myself by watching during my workout time.

8. Protect your time before you need to. When I worked for a national consulting firm my time wasn't my own. I would travel to a client on Monday morning and return on Thursday night. It would not have occurred to me to have made a commitment to family member or friend during the work day. Working at home, though, I was continually doing this, and feeling unproductive and frustrated as a result. Both my husband and my business mentor continually asked me why I was doing this. Initially I said that it was because I had to. But, over time I realized that this pattern was a result of a longstanding issue. When I realized this, I told the people who were making the requests that I worked from 9 to 4 and that I would be happy to assist them after 4 o'clock. This was graciously accepted and my productivity has soared! Look to see where you can you protect your time.

As a Law of Attraction coach, facilitator and trainer I often work with people about procrastination challenges. The Law of Attraction states, "**I attract to myself whatever I give my focus, attention, or energy to, whether it is wanted or unwanted.**" It is important to realize that the Law of Attraction operates constantly. Right now, at this very moment, every one of us is offering a vibration, and the Law of Attraction is matching that vibration and giving us more of it, whether or not we are offering that vibration deliberately (consciously) or non-deliberately (unconsciously). Your vibration, positive or negative, is a result of your words, thoughts, and feelings.

As the definition says, we attract more of whatever vibration (positive or negative) we offer in every moment. This means that if you are continually thinking "I don't want to procrastinate" what will show up in your life is more procrastination. If, on the other hand, you continually think "I am in the process of moving through procrastination and taking action" and you take positive steps each day, you will soon see your momentum grow, projects getting either eliminated or completed, and more of what you desire manifesting in your life.

Always ask yourself: What have I learned about the consequences of procrastination, based on the decisions I made--or failed to make--yesterday? While it is important to not dwell on the negative, thinking about this briefly is a great jumping off point toward correcting your course and developing new, positive thinking patterns. Never lose sight of what is most important in life Ask yourself every day: If I only get one thing done today, what must that one thing be? Then get it done.

Sue Ascioti-Plange has been a business coach and consultant for the past 25 years. Her clients have ranged from small businesses to nationally recognized healthcare organizations. Her services range from interim leadership positions to coaching executives, managers, and business owners. Visit www.lawofattractionforyourbusiness.com to connect with Sue.

Chapter 15
A Decision to Act

by Tanya Brockett

Author: "I have to write a chapter for a book, but I keep putting it off."

Friend: "Oh really, what is the subject of the chapter?"

Author: "Procrastination."

Friend: "Yikes. I guess you will have a lot to say, huh?"

Procrastination. My old friend—or nemesis—I am not sure which. Procrastination may be defined as *intentionally putting off the doing of something that should be done* (*Merriam-Webster*), but to me it represents delaying a decision to act.

You may have seen it rear its head in your life—The invitation you pin up on your bulletin board because you don't want to go nor decline; the stack of mail that continues to grow in height with each passing day like a small child; the late fees in your account because you avoided confrontation in a service dispute; or the friends who left on that fun Vegas weekend without you.

Procrastination can impact us all in various ways. Usually, if you look at it square on, it exists because you have delayed a decision to do something about it. So there procrastination remains, breathing heavy in your face. Sometimes its impact is suffocating. Sometimes procrastination wears on your nerves or causes stress and anxiety. Sometimes it causes fear, which left unreleased can manifest in your body as illness. And why? Because we have delayed a decision to act on whatever opportunity or challenge has presented itself.

Is there a benefit to avoiding procrastination? I like to think of the positive side of accomplishing things in a timely fashion like the pop-up timer in a turkey. Have you ever seen those? They are often these white or yellow plastic circles in your uncooked bird that pops up while baking to let you know that your bird is done. If you respond in a timely fashion, you keep the turkey from becoming tough and dry. Sure, you can decide to delay your response, and you can probably still eat the dried up bird, but it won't be as enjoyable and satisfying. That's kind of like delaying decisions. You may still be able to act on them later, but now you may have fees or frustrations or other negative impacts that make it less than satisfying.

So how do you prevent or avoid procrastination in your life? What follows is what I encourage my clients to consider.

Live intentionally

As the late Wayne Dyer said in his book, *The Power of Intention*, when people live on purpose and stay connected to Source (God, Intention, or Your Higher Self), the situations in their lives more closely align with where they are going. Thus, it is easier to decide to follow the path to your own purpose. This eliminates the fear behind making decisions because you trust the Universe to bring your highest good to you. You can quickly do a check in your gut or heart space to determine if a decision gives you peace, and then you can move forward with confidence, joy, and ease. When you take your ego out of all decisions and allow yourself to be guided, decisions *feel* better. And once made, you can seek favor for effective implementation and positive results from that decision.

If making that decision means you have said no to someone, just do so with confidence and love, and send them off with blessings. *You* are not always someone else's highest good; so don't interfere with them finding it themselves. Leaving them hanging with your indecision may cause them to miss an opportunity they are seeking.

Be an "On Purpose" person

On purpose people push ahead. Allow yourself to be one of them. Having an end result firmly in mind allows you to see the path that lies ahead when distractions or tangents arise. When you are on purpose, you don't have to have the whole path in lights to see that some distractions are not in your highest good. You can then quickly and easily decide not to fall victim to indecision or procrastination. You can decide and move on. That decision may require further action from you or release you from duty, but either way, the decision is made and you can now factor the results of that decision into your next steps. Or you can just let it go entirely.

Take inspired actions

In the book *The Secret Prayer*, author Joe Vitale shares a three-step process for having your prayers answered—every time. One of those steps is to take inspired action. It is my contention that inspired action can also help prevent procrastination.

Typically, when we are inspired to do something, there is a sense of inner resonance. We feel a positive energy stir up inside that gives a kind, gentle nudge to go for it. It doesn't involve fear and trepidation. It gives a sense of inner peace combined with quiet excitement.

When this energy is present, it is easier to decide to move forward because you have an expectation of good emanating from the action. You expect your highest good to play out before you, so you feel better about deciding to take action, and the excitement of only good coming to you is heightened. When you are on a higher vibration, good things on that level resonate with you and bring to you positive results.

When you add to this a sense of detachment—also shared by Joe in his book—you release the "need" for the Universe to prove anything to you (that it was the right decision). Thus, whatever result comes forth is acceptable. Regardless. It is all good. Allow that to be true for you.

Plan your direction or goals

If you know where you are going, you can look at each opportunity vis-à-vis those goals, and quickly eliminate the need to take action on tasks or decisions that are not in alignment. It may be hard at first because the e-mail subject lines are so enticing or the friends can be so persuasive that you don't want to say no. But when you quickly scan your goals and directions, you may realize that the distraction is not just a diversion—it's not even on your road map at all. That being true, it is easier to say no. Then you can allow that decision to be good enough and let it go.

Release the need to say yes or to be swayed

Often we waffle on a decision because we are really avoiding saying no. We would rather keep others or ourselves hanging than say no and move on. We have this false perception that it is an easier let down that way. But really, most people would rather have you get on with it. Decide so they can ask someone else. They will have more respect for you with a no in the long run. (As if what they think about you is any of your business anyway!)

Institute the Rule of Fives

Jack Canfield discusses the Rule of Fives in his book, *The Success Principles*. Others may call it the Rule of Threes or just Baby Steps, but what it boils down to is taking small steps towards your goals each day. Not every decision you make about achieving your goals has to be a big one. Sometimes just deciding to call that colleague to ask for a testimonial or researching videoconferencing services is a simple decision that you can make and a step that you can take toward your goals. Making incremental progress on your goals can help you to keep moving forward so you can keep procrastination at bay.

Mirror your goals

One tip that I once received and I now share with my speaking audiences everywhere is this: write your goals on your mirror in marker. Really. I use a green Sharpie® marker to write my goals, affirmations, or events/items I am intending to manifest on the upper left side of my bathroom mirror. The green is readable without being overly intrusive, and using the upper left side allows me to keep it in the margins and not in my way. Because those who write down their goals and review them regularly are many times more likely to manifest them, the mirror technique gives you an advantage. It reminds you of what is important each day, so you can be swift with your decisions and stop procrastinating. (In case you are wondering, yes, you can just wipe the goal/marker away with a wet paper towel after you have achieved it.)

Allow yourself to decide

When you make a decision to act or move forward, allow the result to be as it is. Don't force yourself to make hasty decisions, just allow the natural flow of events and actions to take place without fretting over the outcome. Allow your decision to be good enough, not perfect, and choose to move forward with ease. It is similar to having a sense of detachment. You can visualize a certain end result you want to create, but don't get attached to how it will unfold. Just allow it to come into being for your highest good.

Maintain a spirit of service

When faced with a decision, ask yourself: "How does holding back help me or anyone else?" Decide to serve yourself and others by taking the decision off of your plate so you can move forward. The butterfly effect of that decision and swift action will benefit more people and situations than you know. Choose to be in a spirit of service by letting go of procrastination and allowing yourself to serve others by your decisive action. When you act in this spirit, it connects you with your Source, which can bring more positive results to the situation at hand.

Like me, you may continue to have procrastination visit you and breathe in your face. And at times, you will find all kinds of excuses for allowing him to hang around. Now that this chapter is written and this book provides other rich resources, we can always pick it up and remind ourselves to let procrastination go.

Tanya Brockett has been a university professor of Entrepreneurship & Book Publishing, and is a veteran small business coach and copyeditor. She helps her clients to capitalize on the power of their words. Tanya owns Hallagen Ink, and is a professional speaker and published author. Connect with Tanya through www.HallagenInk.com.

Chapter 16
There is Science to Procrastination

by Tom Armstrong, DDS

What an amazing coincidence--the chance to write a chapter on procrastination by a champion of that very topic. What more could one ask for?!

This presents a wonderful opportunity to discuss something that many of us have to admit to engaging in from time to time. My goal is to give a bit of insight into the *Why* of procrastination and how this can provide a basis for overcoming a procrastination habit.

Let's be mindful of how truly seductive procrastination can be. For me, and I am sure for you also, it begins as a small thought that pops up when we are contemplating a task we have to accomplish, "There must be something I need to do first." Then another task or project inserts itself into our thinking. This can repeat itself again and again. Pretty quickly, we have effectively put off something that really needs to be accomplished. And there you have it, a true episode of procrastination.

How often have you taken this journey? If you are like many, it happens more than we want it to. All the while, we are berating ourselves because deep down we know we have to get something done, but we have allowed procrastination to take charge.

If we think about it, I suspect that many of us are quite proficient at the art of procrastinating. We have developed our own effective methods to put off doing what needs to be done.

With that in mind, let's look at this fascinating topic of procrastination a bit closer with the goal of taming it better in the future. To begin with, let's ask if everyone procrastinates. In other words, how common is this habit? If you think you are the only person who is "procrastinationally challenged," then results of research will make you feel better.

First, most people are procrastinators in many situations they deal with. A stalwart few, typically less than 10% in most surveys, respond that they are never procrastinators but get things done with minimal delaying tactics. My hat's off to them.

Something like 20% of people are chronic procrastinators, with the potential for significant consequences for family, marriage, job, etc.

The rest of us are in between these ends of the spectrum. Sometimes we get something done in a timely manner or even ahead of schedule, and sometimes we put it off until the last minute.

At any rate, there is a large amount of psychological research on the topic. And it would appear that there are intriguing emotional aspects involved in the process of procrastinating.

One of these has to be fear of actually taking on and finishing a project. Why? Because somehow we think that taking action will lead to some sort of pain. This is often a result of our mind making a future task much bigger or scarier than it really is.

We have all felt overwhelmed with a new project staring at us. How often have you thought there is no way it can be done? When that happens, you procrastinate. But explain your dilemma to someone else and they quickly put it in perspective and help you take the first step. It turned not to be the big deal your mind was imagining at first.

The lesson here is to analyze what you fear, or what you doubt you can do, and then realize that this fear is an indicator of what you really should move towards. Make it part of your action plan that the more you fear something, the more you have to jump in and do it.

Looking a bit further, some suggest that procrastination is the flip side of impulsiveness. Surveys show that people who are the most impulsive often excel at procrastinating. The thought here is that the brain is wired such that impulsiveness is the inability to think through an action first, and procrastination is the opposite. Procrastinators, in other words, have problems with self-control. As one psychologist put it, "just as impulsivity is a failure of our self-control mechanisms—we should wait, but instead we act now—so, too, is procrastination: we should act now, but instead we wait."

Science now hints that these two traits, procrastination and impulsiveness, may share similar genetics. From the point of view of our brain, self-control, self-discipline, and their opposite, procrastination, have the same foundation. Since these traits are so intertwined, the simplistic approach to dealing with a procrastinator, encouraging them to just do it, is not enough. Instead, a more effective method is to reframe large tasks into smaller, more manageable portions and creating intermediate deadlines for these bite-size steps.

Similarly, the process of minimizing our procrastination behavior should also include acknowledging our own particular distraction methods. We have our own ways of putting off a task. It could be reading, TV, surfing the internet, shopping, or any of a myriad ways of delaying getting to work on our goal.

Another strategy to minimizing procrastinating is to evaluate the particular times when distraction arises for us, and developing ways to deal with them.

What this may mean is that our distractions, not the goal itself, are actually the problem. The answer, obviously, is to figure out what our own personal distraction tactics are and find ways to counteract these temptations that move us off course. For example, if snacking is one of our usual means of distraction (it is for me), make it difficult to get up and nibble on something.

While the impulsiveness-procrastination connection is intriguing, more important may be the concept that procrastinators are unable to visualize their "future self" and how one's present inaction will impact them down the road. As one writer put it, "At its core, procrastination represents shoddy treatment of the one person who should matter most to you: the future you."

Many people actually see their "future selves" as a stranger. Because they don't conceptualize this part of themselves, they may act in ways that seem illogical and counterproductive. Examples of this abound – how many people do you know who fail to save something for retirement, are smokers despite the many warnings about the hazards, and eat desserts that their waistlines don't need.

Timothy Pychyl, a psychologist at Carleton University in Canada, calls procrastination an "emotion-centered coping strategy. Many of these emotions are not conscious, so the first step is to have some awareness of how you are feeling. 'Why do I keep not wanting to do this?'" Procrastinators feel good by putting off an unwelcome task, but forget that they will feel worse the next day. Homer Simpson puts it well, "That's a problem for future Homer. Man, I don't envy that guy."

There is no doubt that another aspect of delaying a project or task is the idea that it has to be perfect. Most likely, you are familiar with the saying, "Perfect is the enemy of good".

How true this is for many of us. Not only are we looking at a task that scares us, but now we heap on unrealistic expectations of having a perfect result. This results in a perfectionism-procrastination connection that can stop us in our tracks.

It should be quite clear by now that procrastination is far more than being mentally lazy. Instead, there is a large amount of psychology and likely genetics involved in the manner in which we approach a task and complete it. We might be one of the determined few who jump in and get going right away. Or we could be a long standing master of putting off until tomorrow (or later) what we know we need to get done in a specific time frame. Maybe we thrive emotionally on waiting until the last minute to finish something. Possibly our procrastination habits have had significant effects on our personal lives and workplace performance.

Whatever one's circumstances, I think it's clear that procrastination has many layers, and a corresponding variety of solutions. For some, simply writing down a series of steps will give them the means to finish a task. Others may need to focus on their own distraction habits and address them. Many can acquaint themselves with their future self and use this approach to better handle current projects.

Whatever your particular procrastination challenges are, I encourage you to take this knowledge and use it to better manage your inner procrastinator.

Tom Armstrong, DDS is a general dentist and expert in treating snoring and sleep apnea with dental appliances. He is an avid sailor and bicyclist, and uses both activities to support his procrastination tendencies. Visit www.BakersfieldSmiles.com to learn more.

Chapter 17
Make It Micro, Make It Easy, and Make It Enjoyable

by Leslie Ann Cardinal

If you are a creative, entrepreneurial type of person, as I am, procrastination can be a daily challenge. It is so easy to be distracted from the top priority tasks by anything that looks like it will be more fascinating, or more urgent, or more fun. This is especially true when the priority task starts to feel tedious or difficult or boring.

So I started looking for ideas and resources to help me master the challenges of procrastination so that I could complete my priority projects. I found a lot of traditional techniques that are very logical and linear. You have probably heard these ideas too...like making a list of no more than five or six tasks for the day, prioritizing the list, and then only doing the top task until it is completed before moving on to task number two. Ugh!

I was craving strategies that are a better fit for my personality and style. I needed techniques that would help me make the action process more fun and more energizing, to help me stay interested and engaged to complete my big projects.

Let me share some of the strategies I have found that work well for me. I share them with the hope that you will find that some of them will work for you too. Experiment with them and see which ones will help you overcome procrastination in your own life and work.

Make It Micro

This is a strategy that works extremely well for very large or complex projects. The strategy is to take a very tiny, **micro-sized** step to get started. It's easy to feel overwhelmed by a project that seems large, or by a type of project that you haven't done before. With these types of projects, it's often hard to know where to start taking action.

Set a timer for ten minutes and start making a quick list of the steps that will need to be done to complete your project. Break big project steps into very small chunks. Ideally, make the chunks so small that they could be completed in 5 to 20 minutes.

With the "Make it Micro" strategy, choose a very small step that you could do today. Even better, pick a micro chunk that you think would also be fairly easy to do. This won't necessarily be the very first step in the project. You can often do a micro step that falls in the middle or even towards the end of the overall project.

For example, if you are working on a report or a presentation, start with a key point that that you may want to include in it. You don't have to know where it will fit into the final project. Just start with writing a few thoughts about it. Then look at your list of micro chunks again. Find another tiny piece and work for a few minutes on it. Enjoy the positive feeling of making progress, even just a little bit of progress.

Keep working like this, just doing one micro chunk at a time. Enjoy how quick and easy it is to complete it. See if you feel a bit of energy and a sense of accomplishment just from finishing one or two small steps. This feeling of energy is one of the great benefits of this strategy. A micro step feels like it really is possible to complete, rather than feeling like it is too big and overwhelming. And even if it isn't the most fun task, it feels great to know that it will be finished in just a few minutes...hooray!

As you do a few more micro chunks, you will start to gain some momentum. You may feel more capable of completing a few more micro chunks. The positive feelings connected with completing each step are rewarding and encouraging too. The key idea is to just keep chipping away at the project, one quick micro chunk at a time.

As you make progress you may find that you have energy to do some larger chunks of the project. If so, that is wonderful. If not, continue with the micro steps. Over time, you will find that the project will start to come together. Notice and be excited about your progress. You are moving forward toward completing the project!

Make It Easy

With this strategy, start with the absolutely **easiest** step possible. This is similar in some ways to the Make It Micro Strategy, because this approach also involves breaking your project into chunks. But this time, look for the easiest step that you can take now. It may even be so easy that it seems trifling or unimportant.

The easy step that you choose doesn't have to be the first step in the sequence. It could be something in the middle of the overall project. Choosing an easy step will help you to get over the hurdle of procrastination and get started. Just take the next easy step that can be done right now.

For example, an extremely easy step if you are working on a writing project is to open a new document in your word processor and give it a name. That's it! Then do another easy step, such as setting the margins the way you like them, or choosing your favorite font. Or, you could set a timer and write for just five minutes.

What you will often find is that doing an easy step or two is enough to get you started on your project. It can also help you to get re-started if you've been procrastinating again. As Neil Fiore says in his excellent book, *The Now Habit,* just keep starting, again and again. An easy step that doesn't feel too big can help you to do that.

Make It Enjoyable

The next strategy to consider is surprisingly simple to use and yet it is very helpful in overcoming procrastination. The basic strategy is to intentionally add an element of **enjoyment** or pleasure to the tasks you need to do. I'm going to ask you to keep an open mind about this strategy until you try it, because although it may sound a little bit strange or silly at first, it can be very effective.

This strategy works well for very big projects that may take days or weeks or even longer to complete. It also works very well for tasks that must be done but which are not very enjoyable to do.

The easiest way to add enjoyment is to add sensory elements to the task. These options may not even be directly related to the task itself at all. But they are things that you enjoy and can add by choice. By this I mean adding visual, scent, taste, touch, or sound elements that you enjoy and that can fit with the tasks and with your environment. Let me share some examples to help you find options that will work for you.

For sounds, you can add music as you work on the task. For best results, use music without lyrics. This will minimize the distraction factor. Consider classical music with a "largo" tempo, ambient music, spa music, some jazz music, and other instrumental music. You can find good choices in some of the online music resources, or you can use audio CDs if you have them. You may also find CDs or downloadable media through your local library. Use earbuds or headphones if you work around other people so that you don't disturb them.

When you find a few musical selections that you like, use them regularly when you work on your project. A fascinating thing can start to happen. When you start using the music, your brain will begin to connect hearing the music with working on your project. This can help you to get into a positive mood while you work on your project. And anything that helps to draw you into working on your project helps you to reducing procrastination.

The same thing can happen with your other senses. For taste, try adding things like chewing a favorite flavor of gum or sipping a favorite flavor of tea. Peppermint is an energizing taste and scent, so you could try peppermint gum or peppermint tea. Lemon is another energizing scent. Try a squeeze of lemon in hot water, or sip on a glass of lemonade as you work.

For visual elements, you can put something beautiful or pleasing in your work area such as flowers or a favorite photo. If you work at home, you may be able to have a pet nearby, or you may be able to position yourself to look out a window with a view of nature as you work.

For touch, or tactile elements, try using a favorite pen. This can be a gel pen that writes very smoothly, or a fountain pen, or a felt tip pen in a favorite color. To strengthen the effect, try using this favorite pen only when you are working on your big project. Knowing that you are going to get to use your favorite pen can help you to actually look forward to working on your project.

For other tactile or touch options, consider wearing a sweater or an afghan or a shawl with a very soft texture as you work. The texture and the warmth of this fabric can be very comforting and can add a wonderful positive element to your work. Obviously this is best during cool months when the extra warmth may be especially cozy.

The idea of adding something enjoyable or pleasant can be accomplished in another way as well, by doing a task or activity that you enjoy after you work on a task that you may have been avoiding. This gives you something positive to look forward to.

For this technique, choose simple activities that are easy to do. Some examples could include taking a short walk, playing with your cat or dog, reading part of a favorite magazine, getting a little snack, watching half of a recorded television show, or listening to music.

Another key with this technique is to use a timer. For example, set it for 20 minutes for your main task. As soon as it goes off each time, immediately set it for the next 20 minute chunk of time, and do the pleasant activity. When the time goes off, start another cycle with the main task if you want to. The timer will help to keep you moving forward with each activity.

Procrastination is Not Unusual

Realize that it is not unusual to deal with procrastination. The good news is that the simple techniques of Make It Micro, Make It Easy, and Make It Enjoyable can help you to accomplish the tasks you have been putting off.

Choose one or more of these techniques to try. Jump in and experiment to see which ones will work best for you and for the tasks that you wish to accomplish. Make adjustments to fine tune them and tailor them to really fit you. Celebrate every step of progress as you find yourself letting go of procrastination and achieving your goals!

Leslie Ann Cardinal, PCC, is an expert leadership and career success coach who works with corporate professionals and entrepreneurial leaders. Her Cardinal Rules of Success are a powerful and proven roadmap to achieve your key goals and to enjoy the process each step of the way. Go to http://www.LeslieCardinal.com for more great resources.

About the Author

Leslie Ann Cardinal is a Professional Certified Coach who works with professionals to make rapid progress toward their goals. She has more than 20 years of experience working with leaders and business owners in many industries. She has a unique background of Industrial Engineering, Leadership Development, coaching, and a deep knowledge of success strategies. Learn more by visiting www.LeslieCardinal.com.

Be sure to claim your free resources related to this book at http://TheProcrastinationBook.com.

Let's connect online:

http://LeslieCardinal.com

Facebook.com/LeslieCardinal

LinkedIn.com/in/LeslieCardinal

Twitter.com/LeslieCardinal